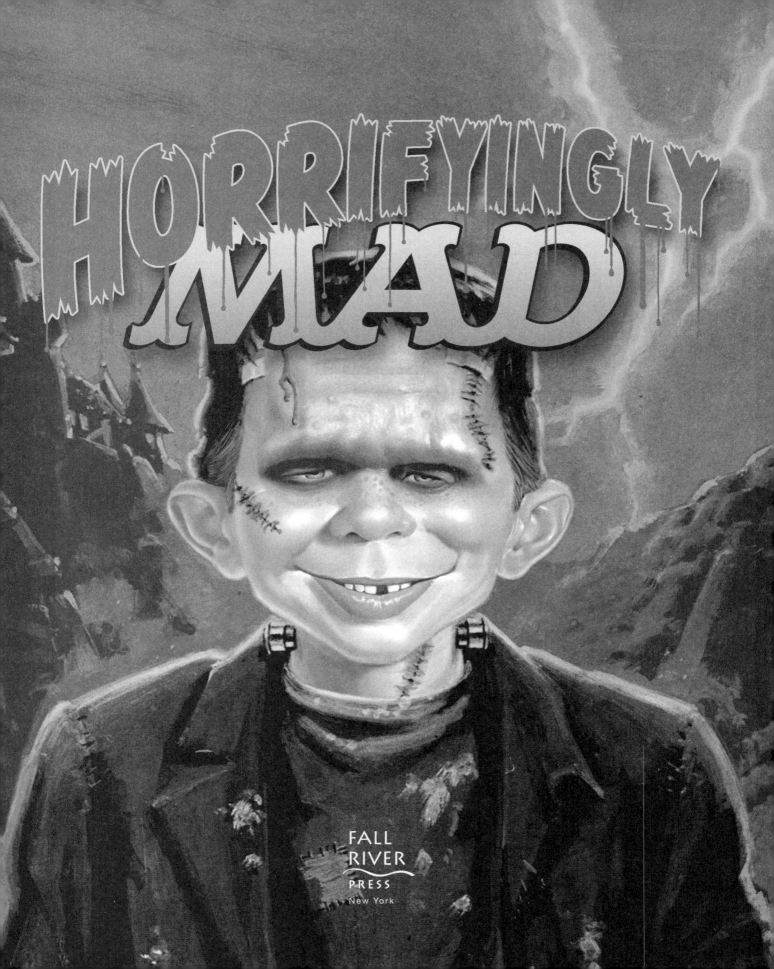

FALL RIVER PRESS

New York

An Imprint of Sterling Publishing
387 Park Avenue South
New York, NY 10016

Cover design by Patricia Dwyer

Back cover art by John Caldwell

ISBN 978-1-4351-3743-1

Manufactured in the United States of America

4 6 8 10 9 7 5 3

Visit *MAD* online at www.madmag.com

Though Alfred E. Neuman wasn't the first to say, "A fool and his money are soon parted,"
here's your chance to prove the old adage right—subscribe to *MAD*!
Simply call 1-800-4-MADMAG and mention code 5MBN2.
Operators are standing by (the water cooler).

www.sterlingpublishing.com

INTRODUCTION

THE INTRODUCTION TO A BOOK IS WRITTEN TO PREPARE THE READER FOR THE BOOK ITSELF. It offers valuable insight by providing a unique perspective, which heightens the reader's appreciation of the material. The very best Introductions provide literary context and relevant biographical information about the author or authors. By that standard, this Introduction can be seen as nothing less than lacking, so let's not use it as our measuring stick.

A less scholarly, but more popular form of book Introduction are those written by celebrities. This kind of Introduction adds sizzle to the overall book package by kicking the reading experience off with the thoughts of a famous person, or a least someone with more name recognition than the pathetically obscure author who wrote the lousy book. By that standard, this Introduction can also be seen as nothing less than lacking, so let's not use it as our measuring stick either.

A seldom-asked question, though one which seems essential to pose now is, "Does *every single book* need an Introduction?" What if the Introduction adds nothing to the overall enjoyment of the book? Or what if the Introduction is a mere string of paragraphs superfluous to the book itself? What then? Should an Introduction be written simply because it's required by the publisher and the book's writers are therefore contractually bound to write *something*, even if it's pure drivel?

And here's another thing about book Introductions. They are traditionally required to be 500 words, which will leave us 235 words short of the goal at the end of this sentence. We could thumb our nose at the entire "book Introduction writing ethos" by adding a meaningless sentence such as this to artificially drive our word count up to 290, but that would be both unprofessional and immature (302 words and counting).

At this point we think it important to make a distinction between an Introduction and a Preface. Let us preface our remarks by saying that we have no idea what distinguishes one from the other. That said, we are deeply grateful that the aforementioned "book Introduction writing ethos" does not mandate that we write a Preface to this Introduction. Ditto a Foreword.

Which brings us to the subject at hand, *Horrifyingly MAD*, a book which mocks, satirizes, parodies, lampoons, skewers and puckishly spoofs the horror genre.

EPILOGUE

While Introductions don't usually have an Epilogue, there is no rule of grammar that we know of forbidding it. It seems to us that putting an Epilogue here is an excellent idea, but before continuing we think it important to make a distinction between an Epilogue and an Afterword. Unfortunately, due to space limitations we will not be able to delve in to this important subject as we hoped.

Since we are held by the publisher to a strict word count of 500 words and have already reached 478 words, we want to be absolutely sure that our Introduction doesn't end abruptly and that we have plenty of space left to

Joe Raiola
Senior Editor
MAD Magazine

TERROR DEPT.! PLEASE! WE WARN YOU! DO NOT READ THIS STORY! THROW THIS COMIC BOOK AWAY BEFORE IT IS TOO LATE!...VERY WELL, RASH FOOL! READ ON! BUT REMEMBER! WE WARNED YOU! THERE ARE MANY THINGS NOT MEANT FOR THE EYES OF MAN! OOOHHEE*EHEEEHEEE*...

HOOHAH!

NIGHT!...BLACK, WET, POURING NIGHT, WITH THE MUFFLED MONOTONOUS SIZZLE OF FAT RAINDROPS HITTING THE GROUND!

NIGHT...ROARING VELVETY NIGHT, PUNCTUATED BY BLUE-WHITE FLICKERING LIGHTNING AND BOWLING-BALL THUNDER!

NIGHT!...WHEN MEN SLEEP AND EVIL WAKES!...A BLACK SEDAN CAREENS THROUGH THE NIGHT, SWERVING MADLY ON THE WET ROAD!

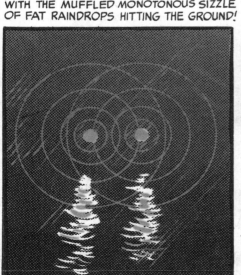

...JUST BEYOND THE LOUISIANA BAYOUS IN THE DEPTHS OF MYSTERIOUS, UNEXPLORED, UNPENETRABLE, STEAMING, SWEATY, DISGUSTING OKEEFENOKEE SWAMP!

OKEEFENOKEEFENOKEE SWAMP, WHERE THE WORLD STOOD STILL! NOT A SIGN OF LIFE... **LOOK, PIC** OR **QUICK!** ONLY A TUMBLE DOWN SHACK PROPPED UP WITH A SINGLE BROOMSTICK!

INSIDE THE SHACK, ALSO PROPPED UP BY A BROOMSTICK, WORKED THE *'PROFESSOR'!*

YES...A MAN WITH A BRILLIANT MIND WORKED, ALONE IN THE SWAMP!

...WORKED FRANTICALLY AMIDST HIS BUBBLING RETORTS AND TEST TUBES!

WORKED AGAINST TIME...NOW *THE WHOLE WORK WAS DONE. THE MIXTURE WAS READY!*

 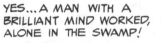  

DOWNING THE DRY MARTINI COCKTAIL AT ONE GULP, THE 'PROFESSOR' TURNED TO THE HUGE VAT THAT HELD THE CONTENTS OF A LIFETIME OF RESEARCH, BOILING AND BUBBLING...

...A RECIPE HE'D BEEN GIVEN BY THE OLD CAJUN WITCH WOMAN! CROCODILES' WARTS, CHOPPED UP ZOMBIE HEARTS, SHRIMPS CREOLE...A MIXTURE *OF THIS SWAMP!*

AND THIS WAS WHY THE 'PROFESSOR' HAD HIDDEN HIMSELF FROM THE SCOFFING WORLD! *"SKOFF, SKOFF!"* THEY HAD SKOFFED! *'NO MAN CAN CREATE LIFE!'*

SUDDENLY THE SCENT OF MANY MASHED POLECATS DRIFTED FROM THE MIXTURE!... IN A FLASH, A LIFETIME OF RE-SEARCH WAS SPILLING OUT THE WINDOW!

...SPILLED OUT THE WINDOW WHERE IT LAY...COMBINING WITH THE SWAMP WATERS IN A FESTERING MISH-MOSH!

NIGHT FELL!... NIGHT ON THE OKEEFENO-KEEKEE SWAMP! SOUNDS OF *THINGS*... MOVING THROUGH THE BACKWATERS!

...HIDDEN THINGS WITH STRANGE CRIES SHATTERING THE SLEEPING CALM OF OLD OKEEFENOKEEKENOFEE!

...AND...BENEATH THE PROFESSOR'S WINDOW... THE MIXTURE CONTINUED TO PULSATE AND QUIVER WHERE IT HAD LAIN...*PULSATED...QUIVERED...AND GREW!*

GREW! STOOD UP! ERECT! A HORRIBLE STANDING GLOB OF SWAMP THING! THERE WAS NOTHING TO CALL IT BUT... *HEAP!*

WHEN THE 'PROFESSOR' WOKE UP, HE FOUND *IT!*...*'HEAP'*, STANDING OUTSIDE THE DOOR AND FROM SOMEWHERE INSIDE THIS *'HEAP'* CAME A CROAK...THAT SOUNDED LIKE...*'PAPA'!*

...FOR THE 'PROFESSOR' WAS TRULY THIS *'HEAP'S'* FATHER! AND AS *'HEAP'* EMBRACED HIM IN ITS SLIMEY BANANA PEEL AND TIN CAN ENCRUSTED ARMS, THE EVIL PROFESSOR GOT A HORRID IDEA!

THE NEXT DAY SAW A TRUCK, CARRYING WHAT APPEARED TO BE A CRUMBLING PILE OF GARBAGE, ROLL UP TO THE DOORS OF THE FIRST CAJUN NATIONAL BANK!

...AND THEN *IT* HAPPENED! THIS FESTERING, PALPITATING HEAP OF GARBAGE SUDDENLY CRAWLED OVER THE TRUCK'S SIDEBOARDS, INTO THE STREET, AND UP THE BANK STEPS!

THEN...LIKE A HUGE AMOEBA, THIS 'HEAP' SLATHERED INTO THE TELLER'S CAGE AND SCOOPED UP THE CASH!... PHEW!

ITS WORK WAS DONE! *IT* POURED OUT THE ENTRANCE, UNMINDFUL OF THE HAIL OF BULLETS FROM THE GUARDS!

LEAVING A TRAIL OF ORANGE PEELS AND DEAD CATS, IT GOT BACK IN THE TRUCK AND WAS GONE! *HEAP HAD STRUCK!*

BACK IN THE STEAMING MESSY OL' OKEEFENOKEEDOKEE SWAMP, THE 'PROFESSOR' WAS SOON ROLLING IN DOUGH ! HIS **'HEAP'** WAS FOLLOWING INSTRUCTIONS WELL !

IT WAS EASY TO KEEP **'HEAP'** HAPPY ! AN OLD DECAYED FISH ...COLD, WET COFFEE GROUNDS... A BIT OF DRIPPING NEWS-PAPER THAT WAS USED TO LINE THE GARBAGE PAIL...

THEN... A CHANGE CAME OVER **'HEAP'**! ONE DAY THE PROFESSOR FOUND HIM COMBING HIS SLIME IN THE MIRROR !

AND THEN, ONE DAY THE PROFESSOR FOUND **'HEAP'** SPRINKLING HIMSELF WITH AFTER-SHAVE LOTION AND FLIT !

AND THEN ONE DAY, THE HEAP CAME BACK FROM TOWN DRESSED IN A ZOOT-SUIT WITH A BELT IN THE BACK !

ALL THIS COULD ONLY HAVE ONE AWFUL MONSTROUS, HORRI-BLE CONCLUSION...'HEAP' WAS **IN LOVE !** THAT EVENING, THE 'PROFESSOR' FOLLOWED **'HEAP'** WHO LOOKED HEP !

IN BACK OF THE PROFESSOR'S SHACK LAY A PIECE OF THE PROFESSOR'S GARBAGE, ACCUMULATED THROUGH THE YEARS ! BY GEORGE...THIS WAS A **FEMALE GARBAGE HEAP !**

THE PROFESSOR KNEW WHAT HAD TO BE DONE! WHEN *'HEAP'* CAME TO LOOK AT HIS BELOVED GARBAGE PILE THE NEXT EVENING... IT WAS BURNED TO THE GROUND!

AN ODD CRY LIKE A STEPPED-ON CAT CAME FROM THE TIN CANNED DEPTHS OF *'HEAP,'* AND IN A MAD LOVER'S FRENZY KICKED AWAY THE SINGLE BROOMSTICK...

...THAT SUPPORTED THE SHACK, BRINGING THE LABORATORY TUMBLING DOWN ON THE WICKED PROFESSOR!

THEN IT RAN AMUCK IN THE VILLAGE... FREEING GARBAGE FROM ITS CANS, UNMINDFUL OF POLICEMAN'S BULLETS!

...FINALLY, PURSUED BY A DRAGNET OF GARBAGE CLEANERS, *'HEAP'* DISAPPEARED BACK INTO THE SWAMP...

...NEVER TO BE SEEN AGAIN!...SOME SAY WHEN THE MOON IS FULL YOU CAN SEE *IT* WANDERING OVER THE CITY DUMP, SEARCHING FOR A CERTAIN LITTLE GARBAGE PILE!

SOME SAY *IT FOUND* THAT CERTAIN LITTLE GARBAGE PILE... AND WHEN THE MOON IS FULL, YOU CAN SEE THEM BEING FOLLOWED BY *TINY* LITTLE GARBAGE PILES!

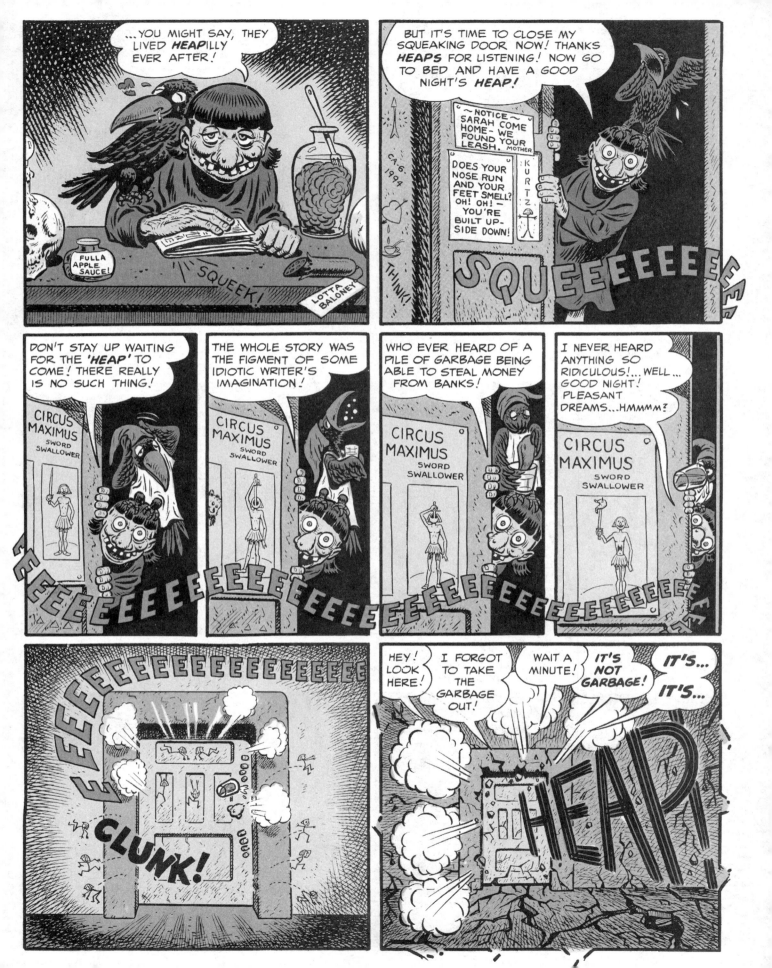

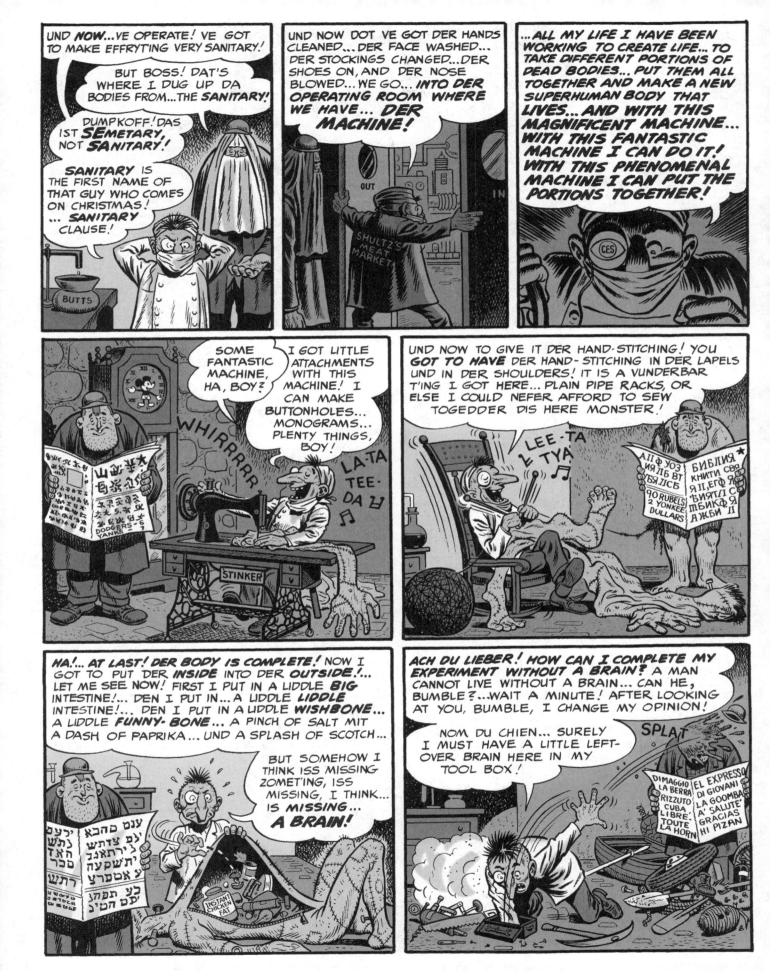

THE RAVEN

By EDGAR ALLAN POE

Once upon a midnight dreary,
while I pondered, weak and weary,
Over many a quaint and curious volume
of forgotten lore —
While I nodded, nearly napping,
suddenly there came a tapping,
As of some one gently rapping,
rapping at my chamber door.
"'Tis some visiter," I muttered,
"tapping at my chamber door —

Only this and nothing more."

CLONK CLONK BASH BAM

That Raven Maniac, Elder.

Ah, distinctly I remember it was in the bleak December;
And each separate dying ember wrought its ghost upon the floor.
Eagerly I wished the morrow; vainly I had sought to borrow

From my books surcease of sorrow-sorrow for the lost Lenore —
For the rare and radiant maiden whom the angels name Lenore-

Nameless **here** for evermore.

And the silken, sad, uncertain rustling of each purple curtain
Thrilled me - filled me with fantastic terrors never
    felt before;
So that now, to still the beating of my heart, I stood repeating

"'Tis some visiter entreating entrance at my chamber door—
Some late visiter entreating entrance at my chamber door;-

    This it is and nothing more."

Presently my soul grew stronger; hesitating then no
    longer,
"Sir," said I, "or Madam, truly your forgiveness I
    implore;

But the fact is I was napping and so gently you came
    rapping,
And so faintly you came tapping, tapping at my chamber
    door,

That I scarce was sure I heard you"— here I
    opened wide the door;—

    Darkness there and nothing more.

Deep into that darkness peering, long I stood there
    wondering, fearing
Doubting, dreaming dreams no mortal ever dared to dream before;
But the silence was unbroken, and the stillness gave no token,

And the only word there spoken was the whispered word,"Lenore?"
This I whispered, and an echo murmured back the word,"Lenore!"

Merely this and nothing more.

Back into the chamber turning, all my soul within me burning,
Soon again I heard a tapping somewhat louder than before.
"Surely, said I,"surely that is something at my window
lattice;

Let me see, then, what thereat is, and this mystery explore —
Let my heart be still a moment and this mystery explore;—

'Tis the wind and nothing more!"

Open here I flung the shutter, when, with many a flirt and flutter,
In there stepped a stately Raven of the saintly days of yore;
Not the least obeisance made he; not a minute stopped
or stayed he;

But, with mien of lord or lady, perched above my chamber door—
Perched upon a bust of Pallas just **above** my chamber door—

Perched, and sat, and nothing more.

Then this ebony bird beguiling my sad fancy into
smiling,
By the grave and stern decorum of the countenance
it wore,

"Though thy crest be shorn and shaven, thou," I said,
    "art sure no craven,
Ghastly grim and ancient Raven wandering from
    the Nightly shore—

Tell me what thy lordly name is on the Night's
    Plutonian shore!"

Quoth the Raven ("Nevermore.")

Much I marvelled this ungainly fowl to hear
    discourse so plainly,
Though its answer little meaning—little relevancy bore;
For we cannot help agreeing that no living human being

Ever yet was blessed with seeing bird above his chamber door-
Bird or beast upon the sculptured bust above his chamber door,

With such name as "Nevermore."

But the Raven, sitting lonely on the placid bust, spoke only
That one word, as if his soul in that one word he did outpour.
Nothing farther then he uttered—not a feather then
    he fluttered—

Till I scarcely more than muttered "Other friends have flown before-
On the morrow **he** will leave me as my hopes have flown before."

Then the bird said ("Nevermore!")

Startled at the stillness broken by reply so aptly spoken,
"Doubtless," said I, "what it utters is its only stock
    and store
Caught from some unhappy master whom unmerciful Disaster

Followed fast and followed faster till his songs one burden bore-
Till the dirges of his Hope that melancholy burden bore
Of ('Never — Nevermore.'")

But the Raven still beguiling my sad fancy into
    smiling,
Straight I wheeled a cushioned seat in front of bird,
    and bust and door;

Then, upon the velvet sinking, I betook myself to
    linking
Fancy unto fancy, thinking what this ominous bird
    of yore —

What this grim, ungainly, ghastly, gaunt, and ominous
    bird of yore

Meant in croaking "Nevermore."

This I sat engaged in guessing but no syllable expressing
To the fowl whose fiery eyes now burned into my bosom's
    core;
This and more I sat divining, with my head at ease reclining

On the cushion's velvet lining that the lamp-light gloated o'er,
But whose velvet-violet lining with the lamp-light gloating o'er,

She shall press, ah, nevermore!

Respite - respite and nepenthe from the memories of Lenore;
Quaff, oh quaff this kind nepenthe and forget this lost Lenore!"

Quoth the Raven ("Nevermore."

On this home by Horror haunted - tell me truly, I implore -
Is there - **is** there balm in Gilead? - tell me - tell me, I implore!"

Quoth the Raven ("Nevermore."

Then, methought, the air grew denser, perfumed from an unseen censer
Swung by seraphim whose foot-falls tinkled on the **tufted floor.**
"Wretch," I cried, "thy God hath lent thee - by these angels
he hath sent thee

"Prophet!"said I, "thing of evil! - prophet still, if bird or
devil! -
Whether Tempter sent, or tempest tossed thee here ashore,
Desolate yet all undaunted, on this desert land enchanted -

"Prophet!"said I, "thing of evil! - prophet still, if bird
or devil!
By that heaven that bends above us - by that God we
both adore -

Tell this soul with sorrow laden if, within the distant Aidenn,
It shall clasp a sainted maiden whom the angels name Lenore —

Clasp a rare and radiant maiden whom the angels name Lenore."

Quoth the Raven ("Nevermore.")

"Be that word our sign of parting, bird or fiend!" I shrieked, upstarting —
"Get thee back into the tempest and the Night's Plutonian shore!
Leave no black plume as a token of that lie thy soul hath spoken!

Leave my loneliness unbroken!-Quit the bust above my door!
Take thy beak from out my heart, and take thy form from off my door!"

Quoth the Raven ("Nevermore.")

And the Raven, Never flitting, still is sitting, **still** is sitting
On the pallid bust of Pallas just above my chamber door;
And his eyes have all the seeming of a demon's that is dreaming,

And the lamp-light o'er him streaming throws his shadow on the floor;
And my soul from out that shadow that lies floating on the floor

Shall be lifted — nevermore!

There are three methods of taking care of trick-or-treat pranksters on Halloween. The first method is to give them what they want, which is cowardly. The second method is to go to a movie and leave the house dark, which is eve more cowardly. The third method is to refuse to answer th doorbell, which is downright stupid because they'll wrec

THE MAD H
TRICK-OR-T

PICTURES BY MORT DRUCKER

Tradition-bound Halloween pranksters who toss garden gate up into tree (1) find that gate shakes down torrent of rotten tomatoes balanced on branches.

Halloween prankster (2) who overturns garbage can is surprised to discover that falling lid removes muzzle and frees vicious dog hidden inside can.

Prankster planning to leave stinkbomb in mailbox (3) is greeted by swarm of bees attracted to honey released all over him when he lifted mailbox lid.

Prankster pulling old pin-in-doorbell gag (4) is shocked when he finds out that he now completes a circuit with the electrically-wired "Welcome" mat.

Prankster planning to hang home-made dummy from roof climbs on rain barrel (5), finds phony top is made of balsa wood, and barrel is filled with glue.

the place. Now, MAD proposes a fourth method, a new way of dealing with Halloween pranksters. Instead of falling for the old trick-or-treat bit, you surprise them with . . .

HALLOWEEN TREATMENT

Prankster (10) is no prankster at all, but actually counter-prankster hired by home-owner to direct unsuspecting pranksters toward traps and pitfalls.

House number (9) has been temporarily changed from actual 243 to 248 which prevents pranksters from remembering number for retaliation following year.

Prankster who decides to remove lower section of drainpipe (6) is shocked to discover upper section is filled with several pounds of chimney-soot.

Prankster aiming to dump rotten eggs down chimney (7) finds it is made of paper maché with catapult inside that hurls spattered eggs back in his face.

Old window-soaping routine (8) gets sudden new twist when prankster finds glass is only cellophane and momentum carries him through into tub of tar.

Some time ago (MAD No. 41), we voiced concern over the dullness of elementary school readers, and presented an up-to-date MAD PRIMER. Now, even the MAD PRIMER is outdated! The single most important thing in the lives of youngsters today is watching "horror movies"! And so, in order to help educate our early grade school kids properly in "horror movie appreciation," we feel schools should offer as required reading...

THE MAD HORROR PRIMER

ART—WALLACE WOOD   STORY—LARRY SIEGEL

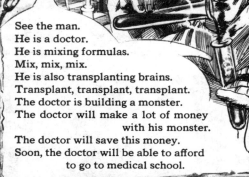

LESSON 1.

See the man.
He is a doctor.
He is mixing formulas.
Mix, mix, mix.
He is also transplanting brains.
Transplant, transplant, transplant.
The doctor is building a monster.
The doctor will make a lot of money
            with his monster.
The doctor will save this money.
Soon, the doctor will be able to afford
            to go to medical school.

LESSON 2.

See the awful monster.
See the bolts in his head.
See how he kills people.
Kill, kill, kill.
The monster likes to kill.
Poor, poor monster.
The monster is sick.
Sick, sick, sick.
He wants to be cured.
The doctor cannot cure the monster.
The monster does not belong to Blue Cross.

My First Scary Reader

twisted little thoughts for warped little minds

by five leading experts in Hollywood horror movies.. Karloff, Carradine, Lorre, Chaney and Freed

LESSON 3.

This is a girl.
As if you couldn't tell.
See how her dress is torn.
See how pretty she is.
Pant, pant, pant.
Listen to her scream.
Eeek, eeek, eeek.
The doctor loves the girl.
The monster loves the girl.
The director hates the girl.
She is a terrible actress.
Even the monster is more articulate.

LESSON 4.

See the other girl.
She is a little girl.
She is not so pretty.
Her dress is not torn.
The monster will kidnap
    the little girl.
She will also scream.
Eeek, eeek, eeek.
She is also a terrible actress.
But she has an excuse.
She is only eight years old.
Then again, she is lucky.
She can always make a living
    writing horror movies.

**SLEEPING BEAUTY "... rousing and animated!"

LESSON 5.

See the other man.
He is the doctor's assistant.
He is holding a brain bottle.
The brain bottle is empty.
See the assistant run with the brain bottle.
He is running to the drug store.
Run, assistant, run.
Why is the assistant running with
                    the empty brain bottle?
Because it is a deposit brain bottle.

LESSON 6.

See the strange vegetable.
He is a giant spinach.
He is big and green and menacing.
He comes from outer space.
Whoosh, whoosh, whoosh.
The giant spinach eats people.
Chomp, chomp, chomp.
The giant spinach grows bigger and stronger.
Little children are especially good
                    for the giant spinach.
They put iron in his blood.

LESSON 9.

See the vampire.
See how hideous he is.
Doesn't the vampire look like Daddy?
Only not so hideous.
The vampire cannot see himself in the mirror.
Daddy cannot see himself in the mirror either.
Mother hogs all the mirrors.
Don't you wish that mother married
                    a vampire instead?
Daddy does.

LESSON 10.

This is a wooden stake.
A wooden stake can kill a vampire.
Wouldn't you like to kill a vampire?
What fun it would be to kill a vampire.
Come, pound the stake into the
                    vampire's heart
Pound, pound, pound.
Oops, that wasn't a vampire.
That was Daddy.
How clumsy you are.

LESSON 7.

This is another monster.
He is an ape.
He tears down elevated trains.
Tear, tear, tear.
He tramples people.
Crunch, crunch, crunch.
He is eighty feet high.
He is tall for his age.
That is because he does not drink or smoke.
Don't you wish you did not smoke or drink?

LESSON 8.

This is the Empire State Building.
See the ape climb the Empire State Building.
The ape hates to ride elevators.
Hate, hate, hate.
Soon he will be attacked by planes.
They will be Spads.
and Fokkers.
They will be left over from old
                        World War I movies.
But his son will carry on with his work.
Being an ape is more exciting
                    than being an accountant.

**THE TEN COMMANDMENTS ``. . . a must!''

LESSON 11.

See the hairy man.
He is a Wolf-Man.
When the moon is full, the Wolf-Man prowls.
Prowl, prowl, prowl.
The Wolf-Man is searching for a victim.
The victim is usually a young starlet.
Woo, woo, woo.
After the day's shooting, the Wolf-Man
            takes off his make-up.
And again he goes searching for
        a young starlet.
Off-screen, the Wolf-Man is still a "Wolf."

LESSON 12.

See the actor struggle.
The Egyptian High Priests are making him
                    into a Mummy.
They are wrapping him in bandages.
Wrap, wrap, wrap.
Soon the Mummy is covered from head to
                    toe in bandages.
When the scene is over, the Director says, "Cut!"
Cut! Cut! Cut!
But it is too late.
Cutting will do no good.
The actor has suffocated from the bandages.

When Don Martin is mixing the drinks, you can rest assured that the results will be "Bottoms Up!" . . . especially when he tries to duplicate the experiments of his idols:

DR. JEKYLL

AND MR. HYDE

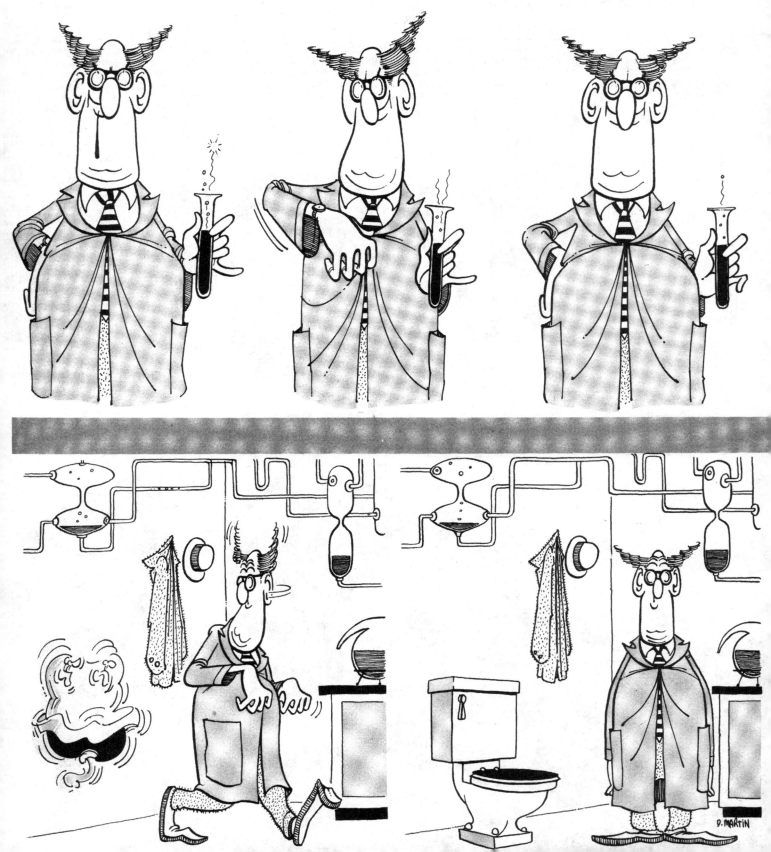

DOWNBEAST DEPT.

YEARS AGO, BROADWAY musicals were all about sweet, nice, young people living in a happy-go-lucky, wonderful world. Today, however, they're making musicals about *thieves* ("Oliver"), *juvenile delinquents* ("West Side Story") *gangsters* and *gamblers* ("Guys and Dolls"), and the worst of all, *business executives* ("How To Succeed In Business Without Really Trying"). Which makes us wonder: Why hasn't anybody done a show about the most unlikely people(?) of all—mainly, monsters? To show Broadway producers what can be done, here is MAD's version of a "Monster Musical" called ...

ACT 1, SCENE 1: The Offices of Schlepper, Schnurrer, & Schlock, Theatrical Agents

We're in **trouble**, Mannie! **Real** trouble! None of the stars we handle is doing **a dime's** worth of **business**!

That's **right**, Mannie! Unless we come up with something **sensational**, and **fast**—we might as well **close up shop**!

Sensational, did you say? Aha! I **have** it! We shall handle the most **sensational** stars in the movie business today: **M O N S T E R S!**

But, Mannie! Aren't monsters sort of—er—**unnatural**!?

Piffle! Monsters—as you will discover through my following song—are **naturals**! In fact, they are **SUPERNATURALS**!

ARTIST: JACK RICKARD   WRITER: FRANK JACOBS

❋ Spooks and ghouls
Break all the rules;
They've got no drama teacher—
Still they're gifted as can be
Actin' supernatur'lly!

Actin' supernatur'lly

Lots of folks
Make corny jokes
About the well-known Creature—
He's got personality
Actin' supernatur'lly!

Actin' supernatur'lly

*Sung to the tune of "Doin' What Comes Natur'lly"

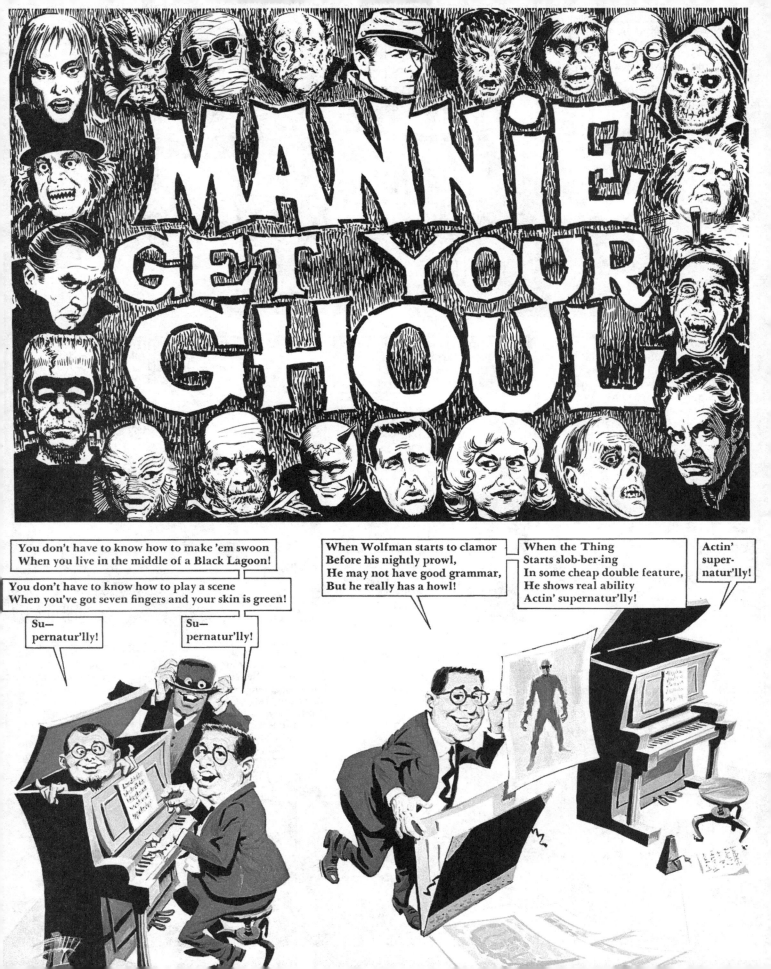

ACT 1, SCENE 3: The Creature's Black Saloon

*Sung to the tune of "I've Got The Sun In The Morning And The Moon At Night"

HORROR Movie Scenes We'd Like To See

ARTIST: JACK DAVIS   WRITER: DON EDWING

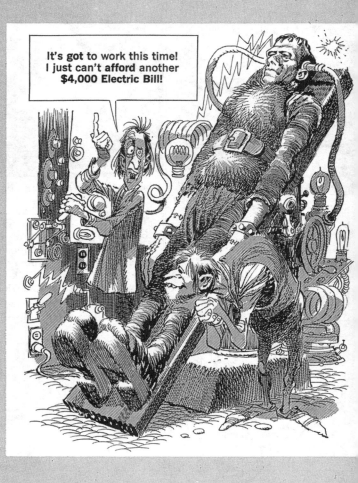

The idiots who invented "MAD Beastlies" have come up with a brand new game. Here's how it works: Take any familiar phrase or colloquial expression, give it an eerie setting so you come up with a new-type monster, and you're playing it. Mainly, you're . . .

HORRIFYING CLICHÉS

ARTIST: PAUL COKER JR.   WRITER: PHIL HAHN

Drumming Up A Little SCHOOL SPIRIT

Delivering A VEILED THREAT

Seized By An UNCONTROLLABLE DESIRE

Burying A GRUDGE

Pulling A BONER

Drowning His SORROWS

Escaping The DOLDRUMS

Letting Out An INSANE CACKLE

Scotching An UGLY RUMOR

Getting A Case Of The SCREAMING MEEMIES

A MAD LOOK AT MOVIE

MONSTERS

ARTIST & WRITER: SERGIO ARAGONES

PLAYING IT FOR SHARK VALUE DEPT.

There's a sick new trend in movies! It started with "Airport", continued with "Towering Inferno", sunk to a low with "Earthquake" and has now reached the depths with the movie that's REALLY packing 'em in, the one about a giant shark that terrorizes a summer community! Yep, it's obvious that people get their kicks out of seeing other people die . . . in every horrible way possible, which includes being . . .

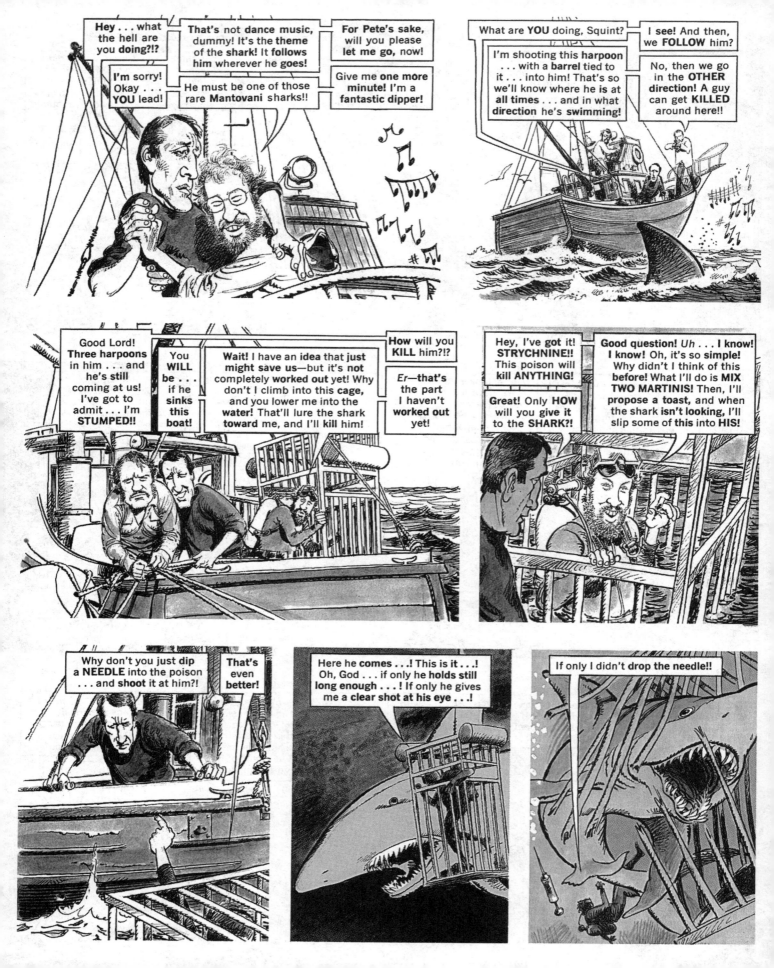

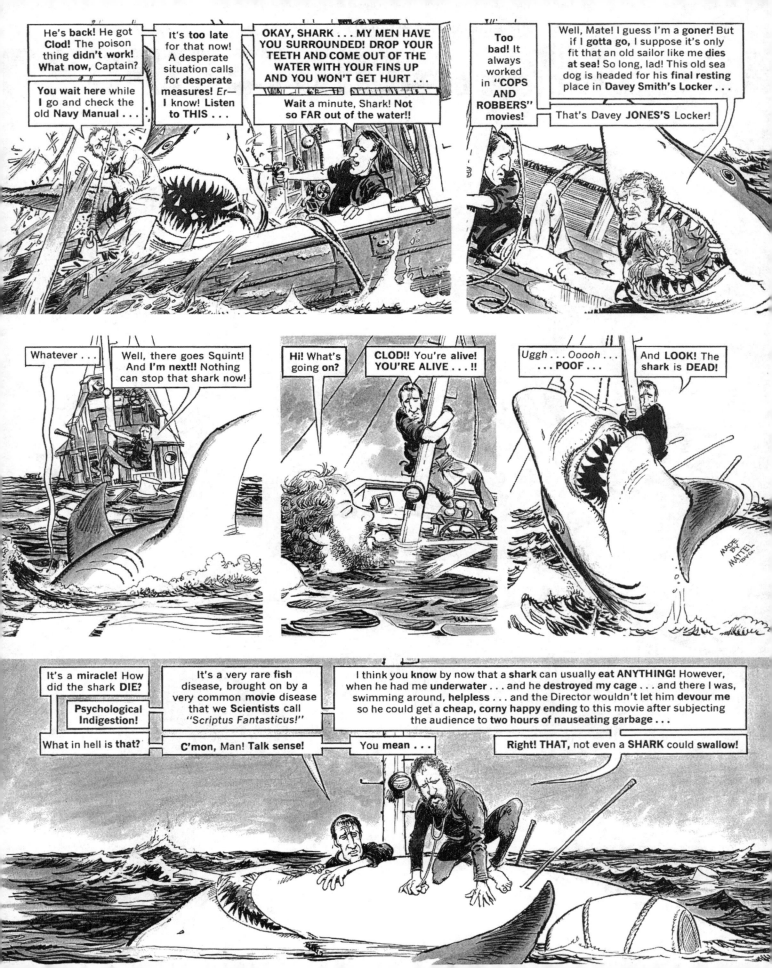

A MAD PORTFOLIO OF... CONTEMPORA

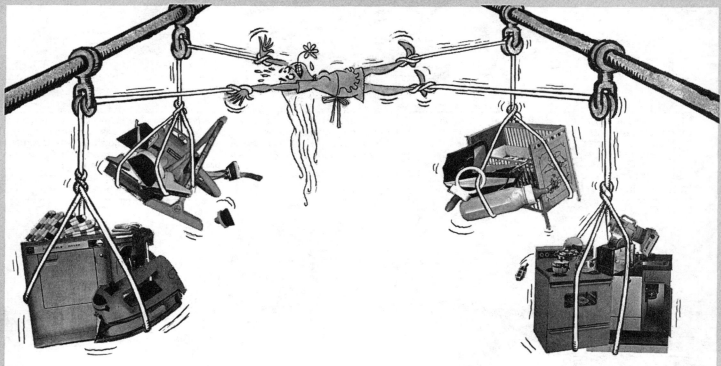

RY HORROR SCENES

ARTIST & WRITER: ARNOLDO FRANCHIONI

Here We Go With Our Version Of A Recent Medical-Suspense Movie.

COMA-

We Merely Raked It Over MAD's Satirical Coals, And It Came Out...

TOAST

Oh, Man . . . it sure is **great** . . . living with a **LIBERATED WOMAN!** No **ties!** No **commitments!**

Hey, honey . . . you want to start my **shower** . . . and get **dinner** going?

UP YOURS!!

Hmmm! And **then again,** there **IS** something to be said for an **old-fashioned marriage!!**

Look at me! A fourth year **Res-ident Surgeon** . . . playing **house-maid** to an **independent woman!!** Why do I **TAKE** all this crap?!

Stop feeling **sorry** for yourself, Mock! Look at **ME . . .!!!**

I **AM** looking! That's why I **TAKE** all this crap!!

ARTIST: MORT DRUCKER WRITER: LARRY SIEGEL

Snoopin, **you** don't want a **Boyfriend** or a **Hubsand!** What **you're** looking for is a **WIFE!!**

Look, Mock . . . I happen to believe in **sharing** household chores! But the **last** thing I would **ever** do is **deprive** you of your **masculinity!**

Well . . . okay . . . let's go to bed!

Did you take the pill?

You **see?!** You **see?!**

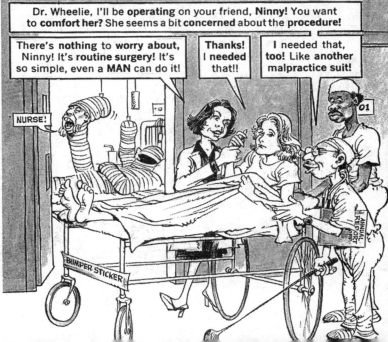

Dr. Wheelie, I'll be **operating** on your friend, **Ninny!** You want to **comfort** her? She seems a bit **concerned** about the **procedure!**

There's **nothing** to **worry** about, Ninny! It's **routine** surgery! It's so **simple,** even a **MAN** can do it!

Thanks! I **needed** that!!

I needed that, too! Like another **malpractice suit!**

NURSE!

Hey, gang! It's time once again for MAD'S new game. Here's how it works: Take any familiar phrase or colloquial expression, give it an eerie setting so you come up with a new-type monster, and you're playing it. Mainly, you're

HORRIFYING CLICHÉS

ARTIST: PAUL COKER, JR.   WRITERS: PHIL HAHN & JACK HANRAHAN

Laughing At A GROSS EXAGGERATION

Shrinking From A LOATHESOME TASK

Hatching A SCHEME

Laboring Under An ILLUSION

Recalling An OLD INCIDENT

Preserving A FAMILY TRADITION

Troubled By A NAGGING DOUBT

Lodging A COMPLAINT

Losing One's Self In One's WORK

Stretching A POINT

W'D, TOO!

ARTIST: MORT DRUCKER   WRITER: DICK DE BARTOLO

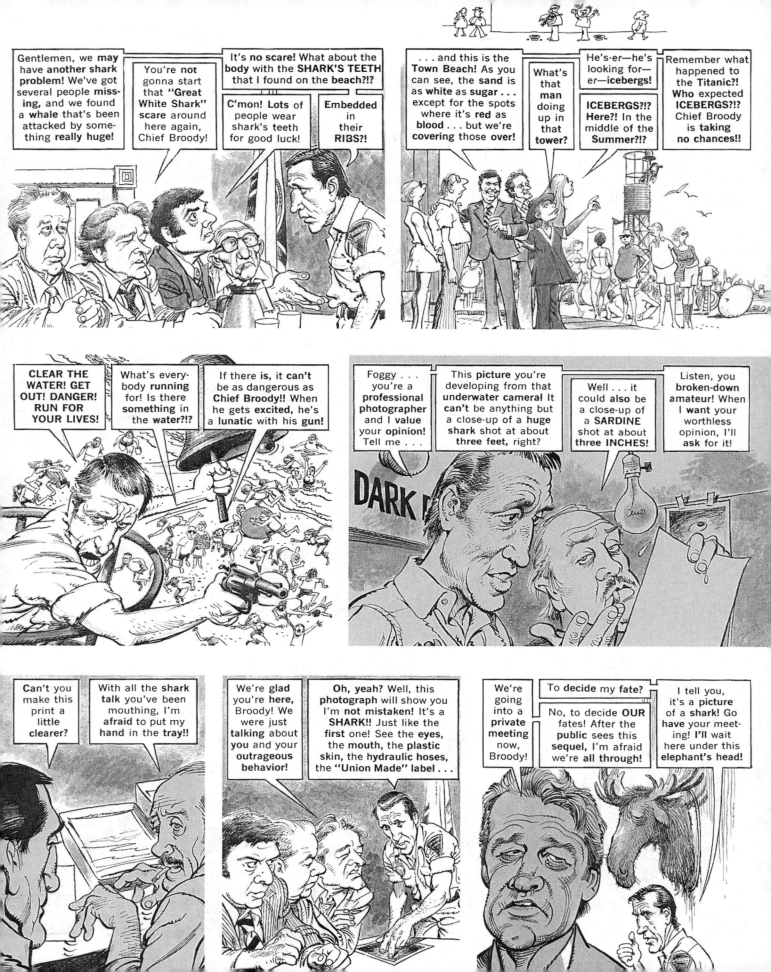

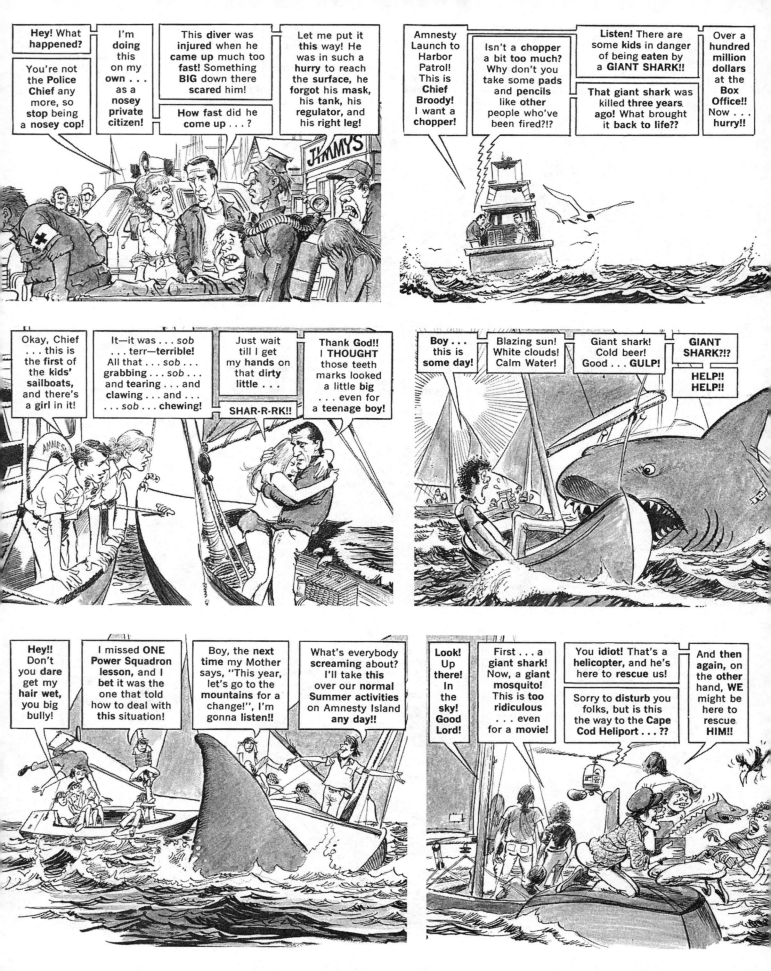

Ever since the movies were born, a popular gimmick has been to state in the ads for suspense films: "No One Admitted To The Theater During The Last 20 minutes Of This Film!" or "No One Admitted To The Theater During The First 10 Minutes Of This Film!" Well, we recently saw a sordid stinker whose ad statement *should* have been, "No One Admitted To The Theater Before, During Or After This Film!" Here's MAD's version of

THE EYES OF LURID MESS

Sorry I'm late, Lurid, honey... but I had such a **terrible fight** with **Ralphie** this morning! **Oooohhh**, sometimes he's such a **snot!!**

Ronald, **forget** your love life and let's get on with this **shooting session!** Say, am I **mistaken** ...or do **you** smell from **MOTH BALLS?**

Well, I **SHOULD**, Sweetie! I've been in the **CLOSET** for 25 years! What did you **expect**, *Wind Song* by *Prince Matchabelli?!?*

Places, everybody! Okay, you **models** start **wrestling** and **whipping!** The **rest** of you, pretend you're **killing** each other! **You** fellows, set **fire** to those **cars!** Ready? **Shoot!**

Holy mackerel! Hey, did you **ever** see anything like **THIS** before?

On just about **every street** in **New York!** Only, **NOBODY!** was **ACTING!**

ARTIST: ANGELO TORRES   WRITER: LARRY SIEGEL

This is **weird**, Ronald! When I looked in my **camera**, you know what I saw? **Inane**, the owner of the gallery, **being murdered** three miles from here! Can you **believe** it?!?

No kidding? You know what **I've** been seeing lately? **Calvin Coolidge** tap-dancing in a **bowling alley!** Listen, cut down on the **Acapulco Gold**, kid! It'll go away!

Ronald is **WRONG!!** It **WASN'T** a hallucination! It was a **psychic experience!** I must get to Inane, before it's **too late!**

WATCH yourself, Lady!! Damn pedestrians!! You never know **WHAT** they're gonna do **next!**

Imagine! Crossing a New York City street at the **CORNER!!** On a **GREEN LIGHT!!** You **dumb broad!** You wanna get yourself **KILLED?!**

KEEP NEW YORK CLEAN — BAN THE MOVIE INDUSTRY

KODAK TRI-X FILM 400 ASA

GYPSY CAB CO

SCREECH!

The latest hit movie making the rounds is about a creature from another planet. It's supposed to be an original film, but it's a lot like an old movie called "The Thing," and a little like "The Exorcist," with a touch of "Star Wars," and a hint of "The Creature From The Black Lagoon," with a slight echo of "Lost in Space." As a matter of fact, it reminds us of so many movies, instead of "Alien," it should be called . . .

ALIAS

Recently, there was a horror film that made the rounds which had as its advertising slogan, "FOR GOD'S SAKE, GET OUT!" Well, not until millions of moviegoers had paid their admissions fees did they realize that it was a warning to the audience—to GET OUT OF THE THEATER before this "horror" unfolded on the screen! But the warning had come too late to save both their money, and them from suffering through

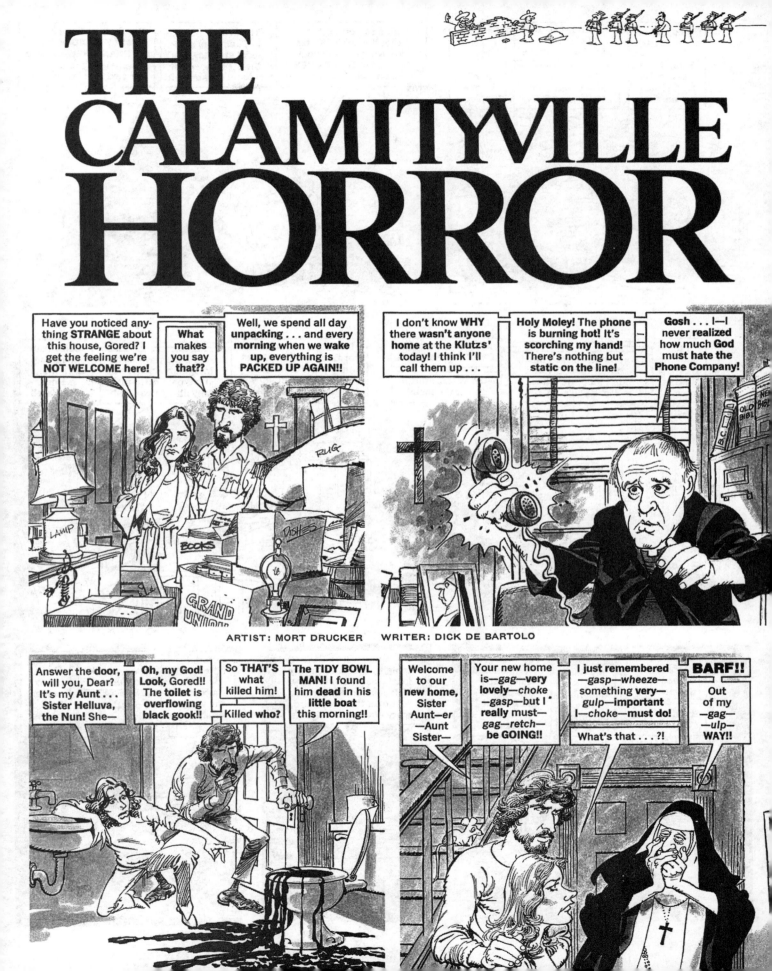

The Klutzs left their house and never went back for their personal belongings. They didn't have to! With the million bucks they've made from the book . . . and a few million more from the movie . . . why would they want any of that old junk, anyway?!

Hey, gang! It's time once again for MAD'S new game. Here's how it works: Take any familiar phrase or colloquial expression, give it an eerie setting so you come up with a new-type monster, and you're playing it. Mainly, you're

HORRIFYING CLICHÉS

ARTIST: PAUL COKER JR.   WRITER: PHIL HAHN

Breaking out of a SLUMP

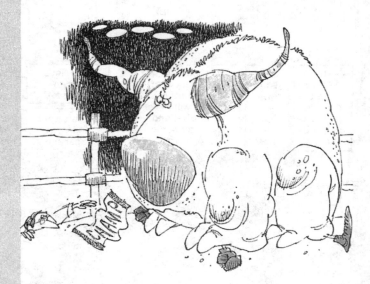

Giving in to a WHIM

Pointing out an ABSURDITY

Plugging a LEAK

Laying out a PLAN

Covering up a SCANDAL

Feeding one's EGO

Couching a PHRASE

Working out your HOSTILITIES

Hitting the NAIL on the head

Everyone is talking about the recent picture that has shocked the nation. (Not THIS nation...Upper Slobovia!) We're referring to the picture that has suspense, witchcraft, sorcery, religious fantasy, and most important of all—a couple of shots of naked ladies... all of the elements necessary for good "Box Office" today...mainly, bad taste! This picture obviously was intended to offend people. If you weren't offended by it...you're sure to be offended by our MAD version of

**MAD REVIEWS ULTIMATE IN HORROR
IN ADVANCE OF ITS FIRST SHOWING**

(In fact, in advance of its being filmed!)

Yes, by George, we've done it again! You'll be seeing this picture in your neighborhood theater sooner or later! It's the logical, if not inevitable, film in the new line of hair-raising, spine-tingling, mind-rotting horror epics Hollywood's been making lately. Remember how you loved the very first classic monster pictures. *Dracula, Frankenstein, The Mummy, Snow-White?* Remember how you even enjoyed all the sequels . . . *The Son of Frankenstein, Dracula's Daughter, Mighty Joe Young?* And then remember how they discovered the Science-Fiction horrors...*The Creature from the Black Lagoon, Them, Godzilla* (a horror in any language!)? And then, how they got real horrible: *Abbott and Costello Meet Frankenstein* and *Abbott and Costello Meet Dracula?* Well, now they're just disgusting! . . . *I Was A Teen-Age Frankenstein* and *I Was A Teen-Age Werewolf!* The next thing you know, we'll be seeing this!

ECCCCHHH,
TEEN-AGE SON OF
THING

ECCCHH, TEEN AGE SON OF THING

AN "IZING" PRODUCTION

PRODUCED BY . . .
Agon Izing
DIRECTED BY . . .
Mesmer Izing
EDITED BY . . .
Pulver Izing
SETS BY . . .
Simon Izing
SPECIAL EFFECTS BY . . .
Sanfor Izing
RUBBER KNIVES BY . . .
Vulcan Izing
SOUND EFFECTS BY . . .
A. Noyes
COSTUMES BY . . .
X. Tortion
PHOTOGRAPHY BY . . .
Dis Tortion
MUSIC BY . . .
Con Tortion
FOG BY . . .
Smogg
BOG BY . . .
Hogg

PICTURES BY WOOD

"EACH DAWN I DIE by Jack Parr

Photoplay by Strudwick Wickerwire
(shown above)

Picture opens with fifteen minutes of fog. Superimposed over it, the blurry credits move swiftly across screen. (They're really ashamed of this one!)

First shock comes when a body without one single mark on it, and without a single drop of blood in its veins is suddenly discovered...in the balcony!

Through the dismal grey fog, we can make out a laboratory with intricate-looking equipment. The fog suddenly clears up when audience yells "Focus!"

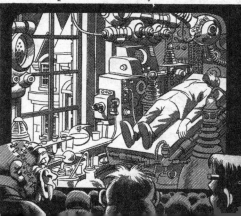

We see two figures strapped to tables. One is monstrous, the other is small.

Lights flash. The equipment crackles. The huge figure twitches...then moves.

It drags heavy feet slowly across the laboratory, hesitates, picks up phone.

Hello, Alan? Failed again! He's too old! No life in him! I need **young** blood . . . **teen-age** blood for the plans I have!

There's someone at the door! I'll call you tomorrow, Alan!

My name is Morton Finster, and I'm working my way through college! Would you like to buy a subscription to **Colliers**?

No! Go away!

WAIT!

Hmm . . . six foot, 180 pounds, nice looking! He's perfect!

Look at my watch, Morton! See how it shines! See how it swings . . . back and forth . . . back and forth . . .

Self-winding, eh? Cra-a-zy! Well . . . I'll dig you later, Daddy-O!

Heh-heh! **You'll** do, Morton Finster! You'll do **nicely**!

EXTRA! EXTRA! READ ALL ABOUT THE TEEN-AGE MONSTER!

Here, boy! Let me see that! Hmmm . . . "High School girl in serious condition . . ."

Hello, Drake Carter, noted Monster Break er, where are you off to?

I've got a **hunch**, Louis Furd! I'll see you later!

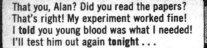

**THE IDIOT by Alfred E. Neuman

Remember how in the good old days, as soon as an actress reached fifty, she stopped playing glamorous roles and either took nice mature mother parts, or she retired? Well things being what they are today, what with the cost of living and taxes, these old gals can't afford to retire. And there are no nice mature mother parts in movies any more because there's something too disgustingly healthy about nice mothers. So what are "Has-Been Glamour Gals" doing these days? You guessed it! They're making Horror movies! They're discarding their make-up, and they're playing maniacs and murderesses. Yes, nowadays, "Old Actresses Never Die—They Just Hack Away" . . . at each other . . . in movies like this here MAD version, entitled . . .

HACK, HACK, SWEET HAS-BEEN"
or
"What Ever Happened To Good Taste?"

Hack, hack sweet Has-Been;
Hear that body thud!
Hack, hack sweet Has-Been;
And watch that corpse shpritz blood!

While hacking, darling, with all your might,
Fans scream all over the place!
It's not your axe that causes all the fright,
It's your own real ghastly face!

Hack, hack sweet Has-Been;
Has-Been, spill that gore!
Keep hacking, Has-Been;
You're on the screen once more!

ROOMS TO LET

BEWARE OF DOG

ARTIST: MORT DRUCKER   WRITER: LARRY SIEGEL

STARRING

OLIVIA DeHACKAHAND	as Cousin Phoebe
BETTE DEVIOUS	as Bubby Jean
TALLULAH BANGHEAD	as Precious
JOAN CLAWFOOT	as Honeybunch
BARBARA STUNWHACK	as Poopy
MARY GHASTLIER	as Kitchykoo
AGNES GOREHEAD	as Charlie
VICTOR BOOBOO	as Papa
JOSEPH CUTTIN	as Selig

WITH

Greer Garson	as a Headless Torso
Ginger Rogers	as a Torsoless Head
Joan Fontaine	as a Pool of Blood

AND
The Gabor Sisters
as
Three Exposed Ganglia Nerves

AND FEATURING
Maria Ouspenskaya as Herself (Right Now)

Hello! I'm Cousin Phoebe! Did you get my telegram?

Hi! Ah'm Bubby Jean! Lawsy, Cousin Phoebe, we were so **excited** when you wired you were comin' to visit us kinfolk of yours! Jus' think, the **one relative** that you like **best** inherits **eight million dollars** in your **Will**! Of course, if you cain't make up your li'l ol' **mind**, the **last surviving relative** gets the money, right?

Well, Ah guess **that** should start this li'l ol' sinister plot rollin'!

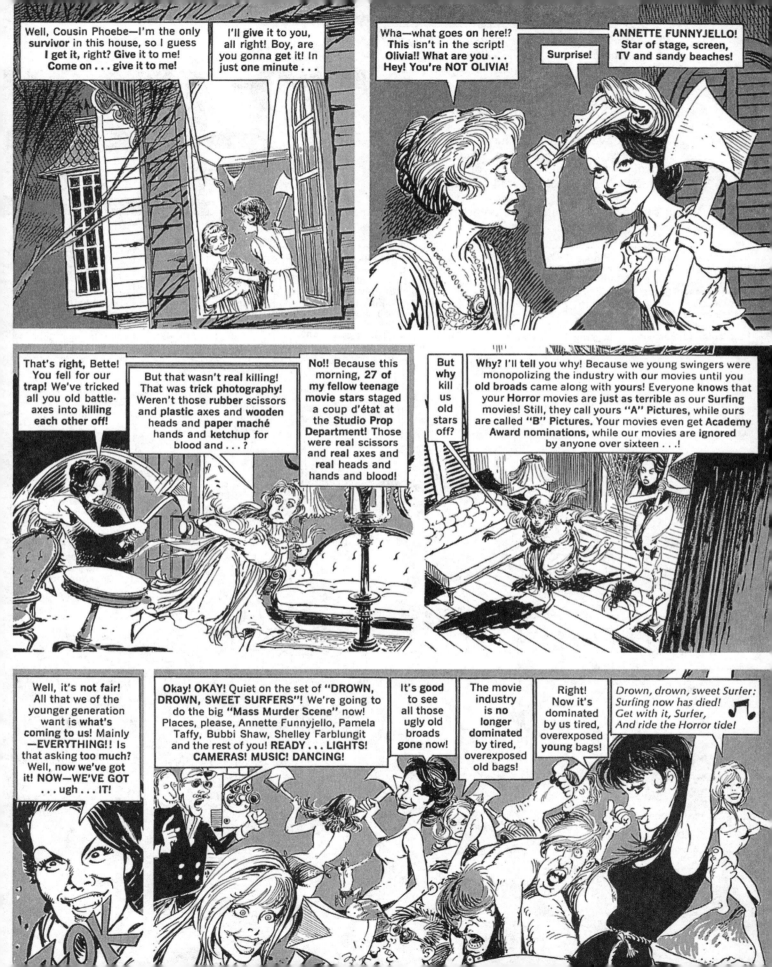

Remember the good old days when Hollywood used to make horror movies about vampires, werewolves, zombies, seventy foot apes and other assorted monsters? Let's face it, they were all disgusting creatures, but there was still something kinda harmless and loveable about them. Well, those days are gone forever. Today's film makers have come up with something *really* disgusting. Yessiree, you screamed at "Frankenstein," you shrieked at "Dracula" and you shuddered at "King Kong," but take it from us . . . those guys were all a bunch of pussycats when compared to . . .

CCHORCIST

ARTIST: MORT DRUCKER   WRITER: LARRY SIEGEL

Hey, gang! It's time once again for MAD'S new game. Here's how it works: Take any familiar phrase or colloquial expression, give it an eerie setting so you come up with a new-type monster, and you're playing it. Mainly, you're

HORRIFYING CLICHÉS

ARTIST: PAUL COKER, JR. JR.   WRITERS: PHIL HAHN & E. NELSON BRIDWELL

Tossing Off A COMPLIMENT

Nursing A PET PEEVE

Executing A DIFFICULT MANEUVER

Visiting OLD HAUNTS

Accepting A GRIM REALITY

Displaying A WILD ABANDON

On The Horns Of A DILEMMA

Patching Up A QUARREL

Staking Out A CLAIM

Getting Rid Of The SNIFFLES

The popular movies today deal mostly with horrible, terrible, disastrous topics—things like killer sharks, earthquakes, upside-down ships, giant apes, living dead people, and swarms of insects. All of

HORROR MOVIES based on

SUDDENLY ... YOUR PEACE AND QUIET IS SHATTERED BY ...

THE INVASION OF THE TRANSISTOR PEOPLE

Don't Try To Escape! THEY Won't Let You!

STARRING:

Barbra **STRIDENT** Debbie **BOOM** Janet **BLARE** Helen **TREBLE** Pat **LOUD** Dorothy **LOUDER** & HOWL Linden

With A Special Guest Appearance By ROCK HUDSON As Gunga DIN

Miss Strident's Wardrobe by Bill BLAST

Based On A Story By Saul BELLOW

Directed By Orson WAILS

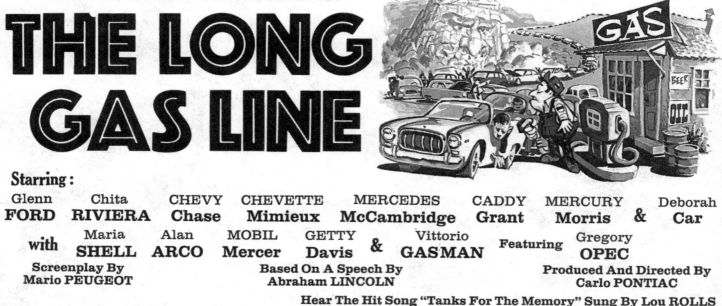

Doomed Souls, Trapped In A Terrible Hell With NO END IN SIGHT!!

SEVEN SISTERS PRODUCTIONS PRESENTS

THE LONG GAS LINE

Starring :

Glenn **FORD** Chita **RIVIERA** CHEVY **Chase** CHEVETTE **Mimieux** MERCEDES **McCambridge** CADDY **Grant** MERCURY **Morris** & Deborah **Car**

with Maria **SHELL** Alan **ARCO** MOBIL **Mercer** GETTY **Davis** & Vittorio **GASMAN** Featuring Gregory **OPEC**

Screenplay By Mario PEUGEOT

Based On A Speech By Abraham LINCOLN

Produced And Directed By Carlo PONTIAC

Hear The Hit Song "Tanks For The Memory" Sung By Lou ROLLS

which makes us wonder—Why make movies about such unbelievable things when there are so many every-day true-life horrors we can really relate to? Let us develop this absurd premise for you with these

EVERYDAY DISASTERS

ARTIST: JACK RICKARD   WRITER: FRANK JACOBS   IDEA BY: MICHAEL J. SNIDER

RELENTLESS CREATURES ON THE PROWL!

Their Watchword Is TERROR!
Their Weapon Is FEAR!!
Their Target Is YOU!!!

1040 PRODUCTIONS PRESENT

THEY CAME FROM THE I.R.S.

starring:
TAX Von Sydow   **AUDIT** Murphy   Irene **Dun** & **SHECKLES** Green

with:
PENNY **Marshall**   Mike **NICKELS**   Myron **COIN** & Lorne **GREENBACKS**

Produced by BUCK Henry   Directed by David LIEN

Hear The Hit Song "Everything I've Got Is Theirs"
Sung by Johnny CASH

"They've spared no expense!"—Business Week

IT'S BACK...To Torment You...
Embarrass You...Disgust You!

UNCONTROLLABLE CREEPING HORROR!

F. Lee BELLY presents

THE RETURN OF THE FLAB

STARRING:
Edie **GOURMET**   Robert **SNACK**   George **GOBBLE**   Robert **GULP**
Barbara **HERSHEY**   Ray **BULGER**   Blythe **DINNER**   Regis **TUMMY**

WITH:
Senta **BURGER**   Oscar **WEINER**   E. G. **MORSEL**   Larry **STARCH**

Screenplay by George **PLUMPTON**   Based On A Story By Rex **STOUT**   Music By FATS **Waller**   Orchestra Conducted By Charles **MUNCH**

"Fills the screen!"—Weight Watcher's Magazine

Human Zombies In A Terrifying World Of Darkness!

PANASONIC PICTURES PRESENTS

DEATH OF A PICTURE TUBE

THEY CRIED FOR HELP— BUT COULD THEY PAY THE PRICE?

Starring :

SONY Bono ☆ G. E. Marshall ☆ SYLVANIA Mangano ☆ Anna MAGNAVOX ☆ ZENITH Bethune

with Don KNOBS Red BUTTONS Lorretta SWITCH

and featuring Adam WESTINGHOUSE as "Black Man"
Screenplay By Gore VIDEO & Truman KAPUT
Based On A Remark By Coco CHANNEL

HE PREYS ON UNSUSPECTING VICTIMS!
RIP OFF PICTURES PRESENTS

THE REPAIRMAN

PLUS

Featuring

Vincent PRICE ★ BILL Cosby ★ Meryl STEEP ★ James CON

With
Bert PARTS and Rod LABOR

"You'll get a big charge out of it!"
—National Inquirer

It Disappeared Into Space . . . Never To Return!

THE LOST FILLING

THE MOST DEADLY KIND OF FALL OUT!

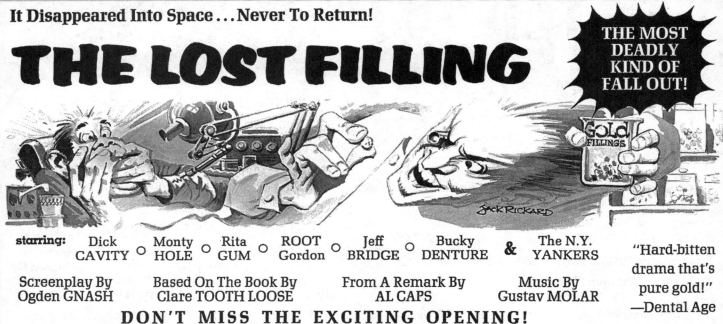

starring: Dick CAVITY ○ Monty HOLE ○ Rita GUM ○ ROOT Gordon ○ Jeff BRIDGE ○ Bucky DENTURE & The N.Y. YANKERS

Screenplay By Ogden GNASH

Based On The Book By Clare TOOTH LOOSE

From A Remark By AL CAPS

Music By Gustav MOLAR

"Hard-bitten drama that's pure gold!"
—Dental Age

DON'T MISS THE EXCITING OPENING!

A long time ago, they made a movie about a Psycho who poisoned his mother and then hacked up a few other people. In the end, he was put into a hospital for the criminally insane. But after twenty years, they released him so he could commit an even more disgusting crime...making this sequel to that first movie! But this time around, he's not the only weird one. He's surrounded by several women who are...

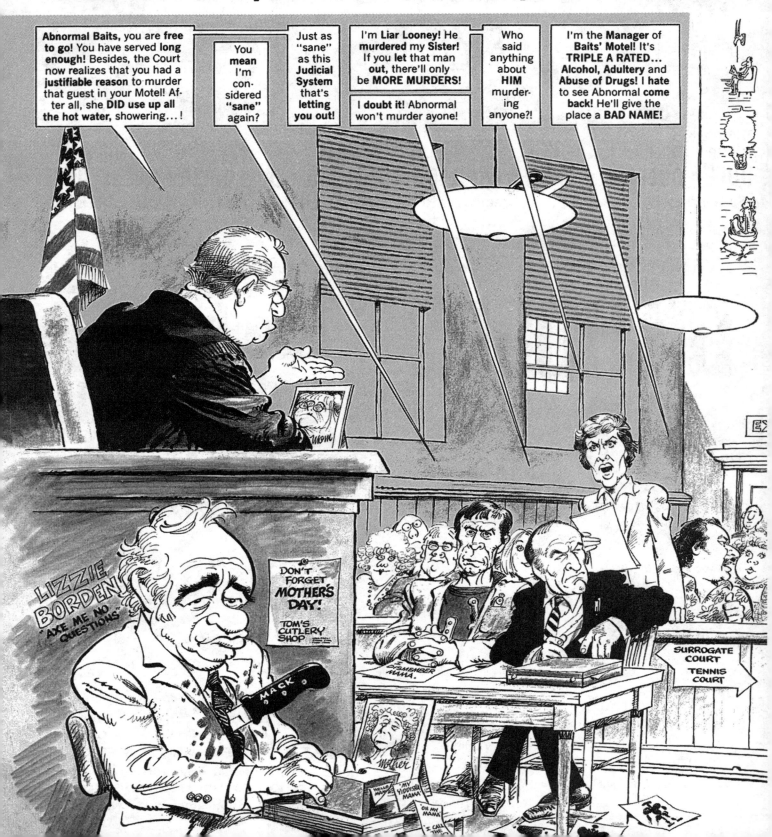

PSYCHO, TOO

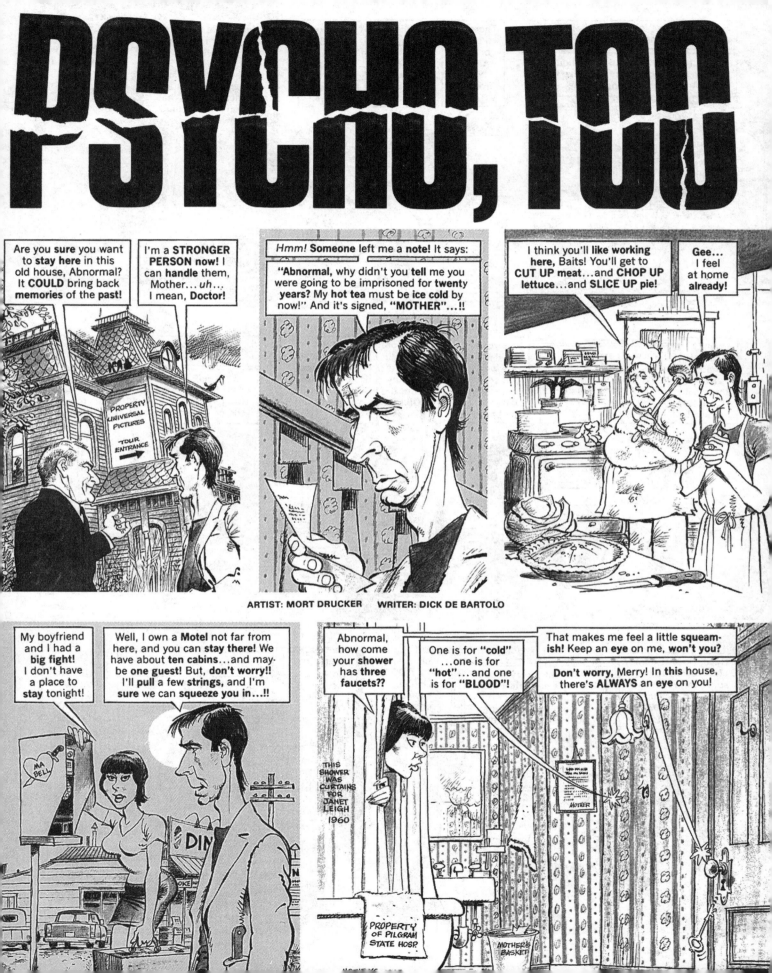

ARTIST: MORT DRUCKER   WRITER: DICK DE BARTOLO

A Mad Look At "Nightmare On

Elm Street"

ARTIST AND WRITER: SERGIO ARAGONES   "FREDDY" BY: KEVIN YAGHER

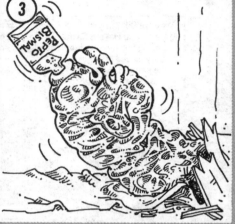

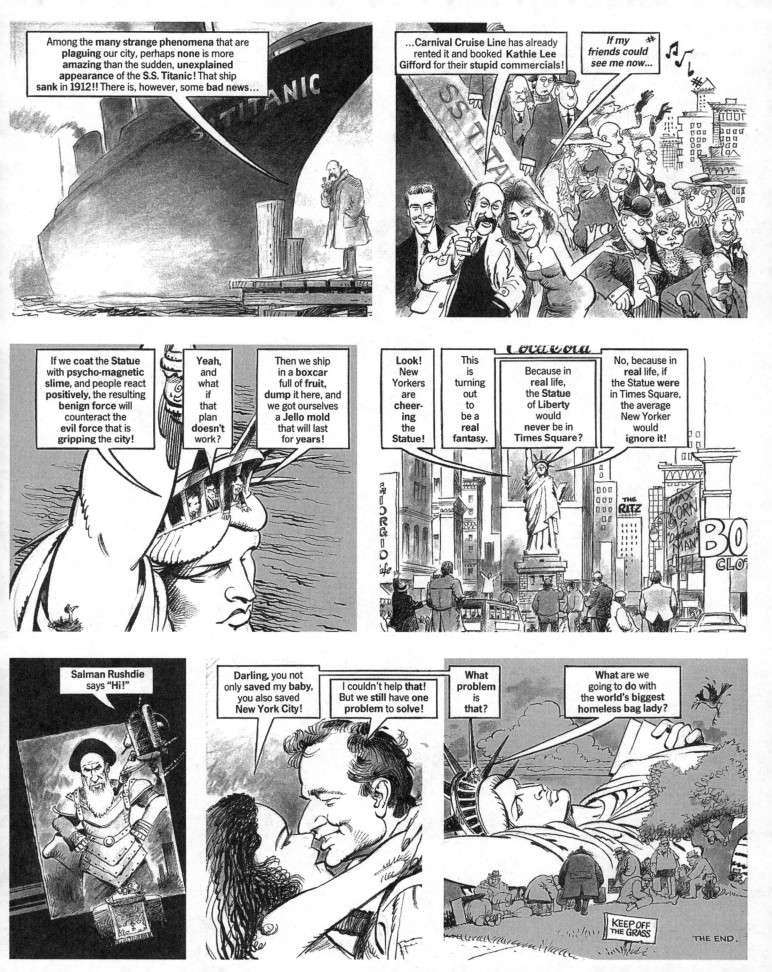

Hey, gang! It's time once again for MAD'S new game. Here's how it works: Take any familiar phrase or colloquial expression, give it an eerie setting so you come up with a new-type monster, and you're playing it. Mainly, you're

HORRIFYING CLICHÉS

ARTIST: PAUL COKER, JR.   WRITERS: PHIL HAHN, GEORGE WOODBRIDGE & MAY SAKAMI

Bowing To The INEVITABLE

Fighting A MONSTROUS INJUSTICE

Picking The Lesser Of TWO EVILS

Heaving A SIGH

Taking A CALCULATED RISK

Protecting A SLIM LEAD

Unearthing A FOUL PLOT

Whipping Up A FRENZY

Stifling A YAWN

Ignoring A SNIDE REMARK

Every once in a while, a new movie comes along that's funny, clever and in good taste. Maybe one day we'll be lucky enough to see one! Until then, we'll just have to take whatever Hollywood throws up to us as we try to stomach…

THE WRETCHES OF ECCHFLICK

I'm **Spookie Witchmeat!** In college I **majored** in **fertility!** My husband **left me** because every time we had **sex** I got **pregnant!** How fertile **am I?** I **gave birth** on the **first date!**

I'm **Jade Boffer!** I teach music at the local school! I used to lack **self-esteem**, but **Drool's changed all that!** He's filled me with so much **lust** and **desire** that now I'm **proud** to be a **bimbo!**

I'm **Abracadabra Bedbird**, one of Drool's **sexual conquests!** To me, he's **gross, vulgar, sickening** and **emotionally retarded!** Lucky for him I'm a **pushover** for men who are **gross, vulgar, sickening** and **emotionally retarded!**

I'm **Drool Van Horny**, but my friends call me **Satan!** I'm Ecchflick's one and only **sex-crazed, supernatural weirdo!** I love flaunting my **wealth** and **power**, and when I don't get what I want, I **plead** and **whine** and **carry on** something awful until they **come across!** The way I see it, if I **bomb out** here, I can always make it as a **televangelist!**

AT LAST DE TAIL!

ARTIST: MORT DRUCKER   WRITER: FRANK JACOBS

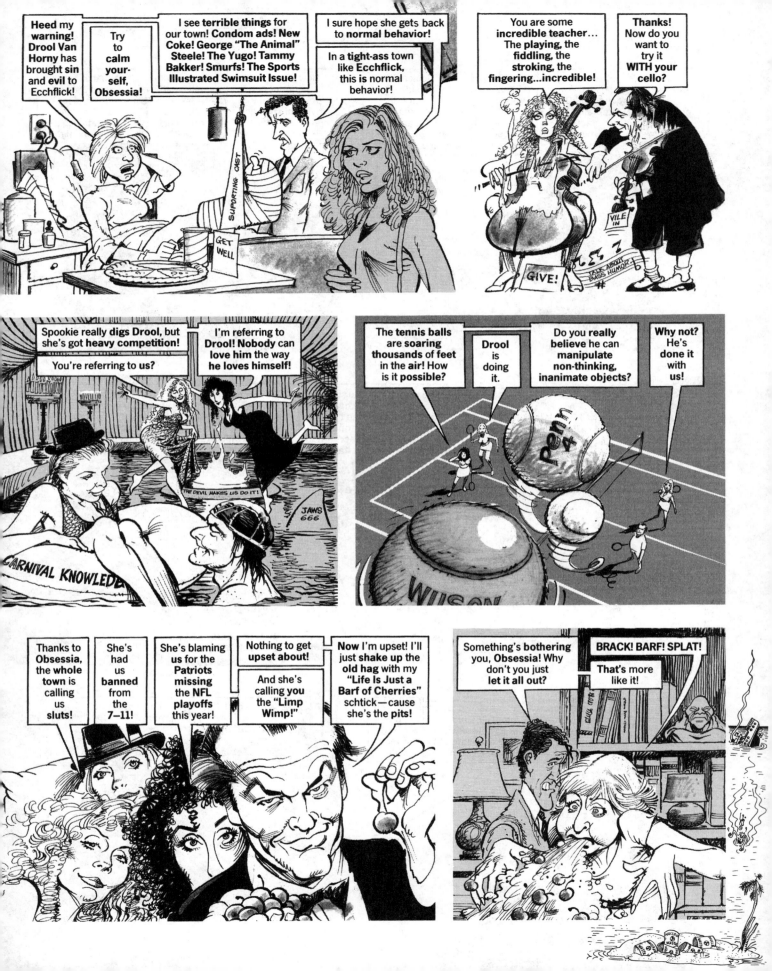

We thought we were lucky. After *Alien³* tanked a few years back, we were sure that those schmucks in Hollywood wouldn't want to foist another crappy installment of their gory series on us. Man, were we wrong! Instead, they pumped some stale air into a bad script, and we got...

ALI
RESUSCI

MOrt DRUCKER

I'm **Ripple!** Let me give you a **little background** — I was a hero at the end of *Alien³*, and I was also **dead!** And "**dead**" is about as "**hero**" as you **can get!** Thanks to advanced **DNA cloning,** the doctors — **script doctors,** that is — were able to take a **formerly closed** *Alien* movie trilogy and **breathe life** back into it for **this,** and at least **one more,** feature! I just hope it does **better** than *Rocky IV* and *V!*

I'm **Dr. Mayhem Wrench!** The **new alien** I cloned from Ripple presents a **wonderful opportunity** for **inter-action!** I'm positive we can **teach** them our **human ways** by using advanced **logic** and **kindness!** Then, after **15 seconds,** if they **haven't responded** the way I want, we can resort to my favorite **old-fashioned methods** — heavy-duty **S&M treatment!**

I'm **General Putz** and I'm in charge of this **secret mission!** I sort of hoped that as **General,** I'd know what the mission is, but basically it's so **top secret** my orders are to just **float around** in space till the **closing credits** or I **die,** whichever comes first!

We're **futuristic pirates** — ruthless **scumbags** who will do **anything** to **raise cash!** We used to work for **America Online,** but now that **every earthling** has been **duped** into **signing up,** we've set out **on our own** to **dupe** and screw **entire galaxies!**

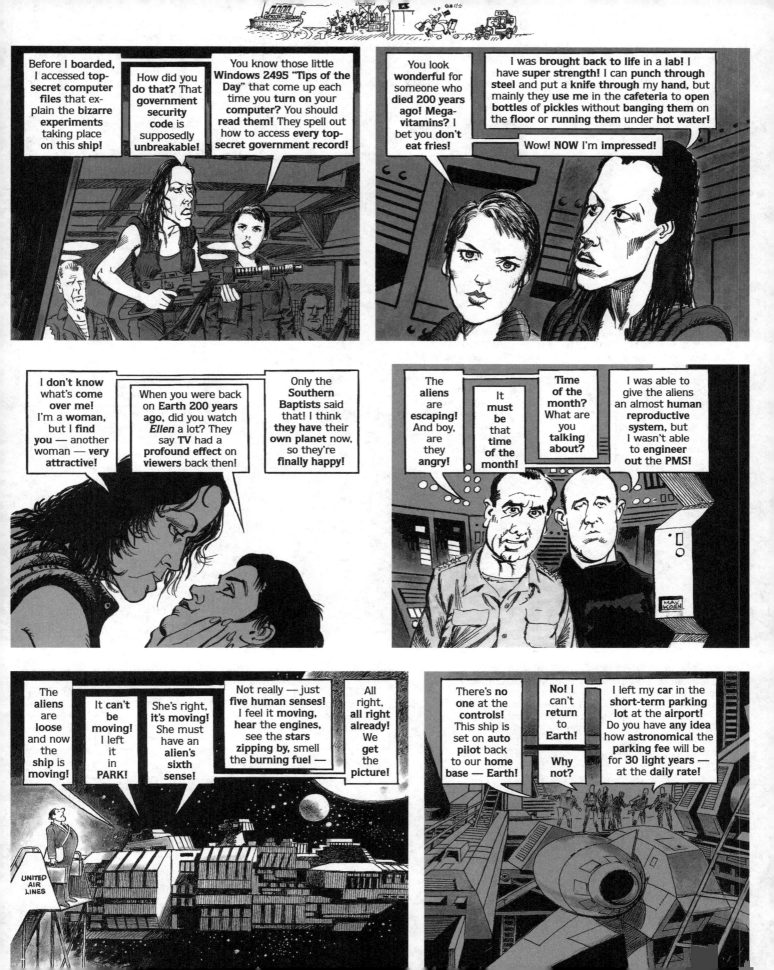

Thank you, thank you very much! The King here — since I'm the most famous ghost around, MAD tracked me down at a séance and begged me to review this movie! They thought first of asking Patrick Swayze, since he starred in the movie *Ghost,* but he's still alive — although you couldn't tell by his acting! Thank you, thank you very much! Anyway, allow me to introduce...

GASPER

ARTIST: PAUL COKER   WRITER: STAN HART

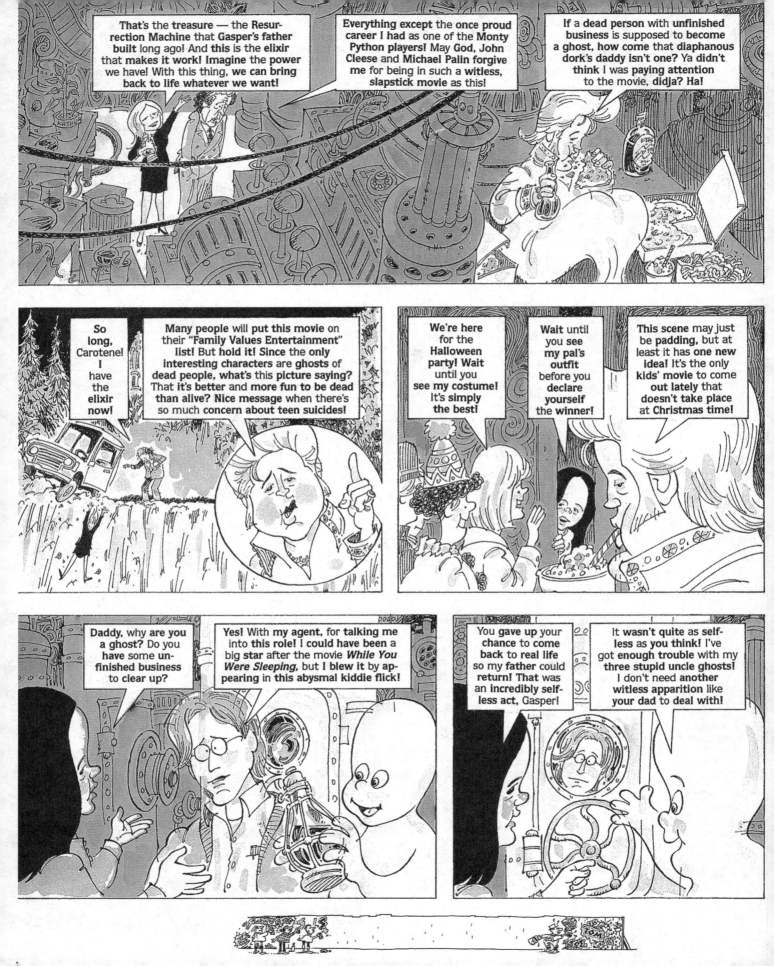

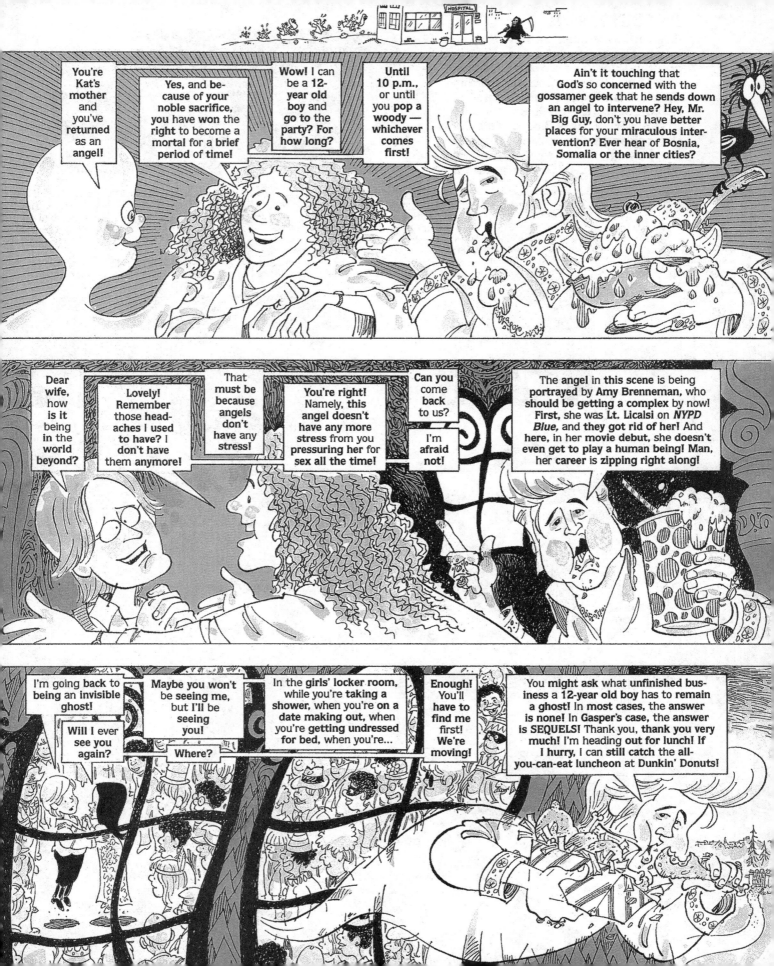

A talented writer named Steven King once wrote a terrifying book called "The Shining." Now, a famous Director named Stanley Kubrick has made a movie out of it. Unfortunately, his film has given Mr. King's book, and all the other great horror films of the past, a black eye! Which is why we at MAD call our version:

THE

ARTIST: DON MARTIN   WRITER: DON EDWING

As you've probably noticed, there are a lot of horror movies around these days. The reason for this is: horror movies make big money! Modern horror films differ from the old Frankenstein-Dracula-type flicks because of changes in taste. Today's movie-goers are weaned on TV violence: Saturday Morning Cartoons, Monday Night Football and the Seven O'clock News. They demand plenty of blood, graphic mutilations and all the other yecchy stuff found in films like . . .

ARBO

Hi, there, horror buffs! I'm **Gore Gruesome**, film maker! Before we screen my **latest epic**, I'd like to set the record straight! Contrary to popular belief, horror movies are **not** cheap to make! Hey, have you checked out the price of Ketchup lately? Man, it would be cheaper to use **real blood**! Many Psychologists claim that horror movies are **harmful** . . . and it's **true**! They ARE if they **bomb** at the **box office**! Then, they're not only **harmful**— they're **fatal**! Especially if you're the **Producer**! But now it's showtime! Sit back, relax, and enjoy this preview of my latest release, **"Arbor Day"** . . .

Okay, so **"Arbor Day"** doesn't exactly give you **goosebumps**! But all the **real scary titles** like **"Friday The 13th," "Prom Night," "Easter Sunday," "New Year's Eve," "Halloween"** and **"Mother's Day"** have been **used**!

Now, when you make a horror movie **today**, the idea is to **gross out the audience** right at the **start**! Kids judge horror movies by their **"barf power"** so you gotta get 'em to lose their popcorn **early**! A nice, gory **chain saw slaughter** always works!

R DAY

ARTIST: JACK DAVIS
WRITER: LOU SILVERSTONE

Yep, a **chain saw** becomes an **instrument** of **terror** when you turn up the **sound** to a **deafening pitch** and show it slowly approaching a **terrified girl!** Then, you spatter the screen with **blood** and **severed limbs,** and the movie theater is filled with **hysterical shrieks** . . .

. . . usually from the **angry USHERS** . . . who are screaming because some **idiot** just **barfed** all over the **floor** . . . and **they're** gonna have to **clean** it up!!

After the **gory opening scene,** we get to the alleged **plot!** A group of **nubile coeds** have to find some **stupid reason** to visit a **frightening place** where they can be **terrorized** and **slaughtered!** Having this scene played in the **semi-nude** doesn't add anything to the **plot,** but it'll get us an **"R" rating,** and we'll **need** that if we want the **kids** to come and see the movie!

YAAAHH!
PRRR!

Hey, gang!! It's **ARBOR DAY!** Let's all go into **Demon Forest** and **plant** some **trees!**

Forget it! If we **go** into those woods, **WE** might be what gets **planted!**

Ahh, you're being **silly!** Just because **13 girls** disappeared **LAST Arbor Day** is no reason to act like **scared children!**

Oh, **yeah!!** Well, I'm **STILL** scared!!

You'll notice that there's never much **dialogue** in horror movies, for which the **audience** can be grateful! I mean . . . why hire a **writer** to type up a bunch of **dumb** lines when **I** can do the **same thing myself?!**

Another reason to keep the dialogue to a minimum is we use **young actors** who **can't act!** It really **doesn't matter** as long as the girls are **pretty** and **sexy**, the boys are **handsome** . . . and mainly they can all **scream!**

I wonder where the **boys** are! It's not like them to be **late** for a **makeout date** with us!

Gee! Maybe they got **tied up!**

I'll bet that they're **play**ing a **trick** on us! You know what **cut**ups they are!

Can you girls **keep** it **down?** It's **hard** enough reading the plays of Aristophanes without all that silly **chatter!**

HALLLP YAAAA!

I really don't like to **complain**, but producing a horror film is a **real challenge!** You give the audience **dismemberment** and **mutilations** . . . and **still** they aren't **satisfied!** They want **more . . . more . . .**

So I give 'em **more . . . more . . . !** The **latest** successful horror movie gimmick is **"cannibalism,"** and **this** little offering of mine has a **healthy portion** of it! **Hmm! I** hate to think what they'll come up with **next!**

Oh, **Sonny!** You're back from the **horsepistol** and you brung your Ma some **nice fresh meat!**

Well, f'r bein' such a **good boy**, I'm gonna make you a **nice Kidney Pie!!**

This **roadside restaurant** is run by **Druid's** mother! I'm hoping she's seen him . . . !

I'm **starving . . . !** How's the **food??**

It's like **nothing you** ever tasted!

MOM'S PIZZAS

OPEN

HOME MADE KIDNEY PIES!

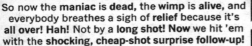

Now comes the *piece de résistance* . . . the **final shock effect** . . . a **spectacular touch** that **ties up** with the **Arbor Day** theme! As the old lady chases our heroine into the storm, she gets **crushed** by a falling tree!

YOU KILLED MY BABY!! YOU KILLED MY BABY!! LOOK WHAT YOU **DID** TO HIM!!

JUST BECAUSE HE HAD A **SPLIT PERSONALITY** . . . YOU DIDN'T HAVE TO GO AND **PROVE** IT!!

ZAP

AAAAGHH

Are you all right, Miss Wimp?

I'm **okay**, but the **others** are all **dead**! **Chopped meat**! It seems that **Druid Acorn** was supplying his **Mom** with meat to keep her **restaurant** in **business** so she wouldn't have to **sell out** to those **developers**!

You mean th-those **pizzas** we ate had . . . **GAACCK!**

No need to **worry**—gasp— Sheriff! At least there weren't any **chemicals** or **preservatives** in 'em— gasp! Just **fresh meat**— gasp! Happy Arbor Day!

And **that's it!** I'd like to **stay** and **rap**, but I've **got** to start work on my **latest horror flick!** It's called "**Ground Hog Day**" . . . and it's about a group of **coeds** who go into the **woods** to see if the **ground hog** comes up and sees his **shadow**, and there's this **crazed naturalist** with a **machete** . . . but why **spoil** it for you!? You can all **see** it in your **local theaters** in about **three weeks!** In the meantime . . . **Ciao!**

MODERN UPDATED TALES FROM THE CRYPT

ARTIST: GREG THEAKSTON   WRITER: RUSS COOPER

Hoo! HOY! Howdy, VULGAR VAULT-VOGUERS! Ready for a little HORROR HANKY PANKY, a sensual slice o' FEAR-OTICA? (PANT!) Papa don't SCREECH, 'cause it's time for a little Truth or SCARE! But there's only one BOY TOY who wishes a certain MATERIAL GHOUL was still LIKE A VIRGIN! It's no HOLIDAY when time comes for him to EXPRESS HIMSELF by YOWLING in DOOMED DESPERATION...

I AM MADONNA'S GYNECOLOGIST!

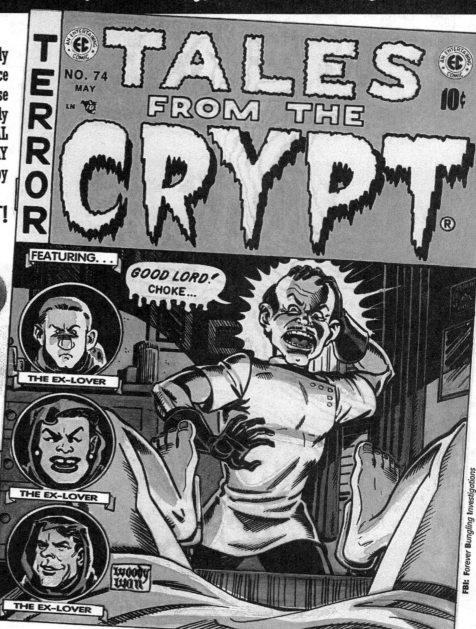

No time for a SPOOKY intro, dear FEAR-ENGIS! We've got a DEADLINE to meet! A Special GHOUL-LETIN, this just GRIM! FEAR now, our TOP GORY...INFIRMED SOURCES tell us that the latest issue of NEWS-REEK predicts a surprising REVELATION that's supported by TED KOP-HELL on the next DEAD-ition of PRIMETIME DEAD! It's a huge price TOUPEE, but somebody has to finally expose the HORRIFYING HAIR-VARNISHING SECRET of...

THE THING ON SAM DONALDSON'S HEAD!

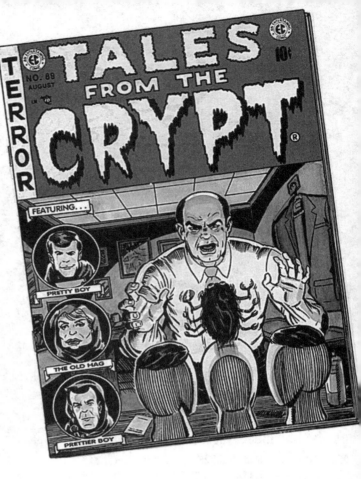

Heh! Heh! BONE appetit, FIENDS! It's your DEAD WAITER, the CRYPT-KEEPER, and I've got quite a TASTY tale COOKED up for all you a-FISHER-ionados! This story takes place at a small LONG ISLAND diner, the SORDID setting for an UNGODLY number of MEDIOCRE Made-for-TV movies! A SPINE-TINGLING, FINGER-LICKING evening with a DEADLY DISH, and BEREAVE ME, a date like this you need like a HOLE in the HEAD! (Burp!) So settle down for this latest SERVING from the on-going BUTTAFUOCO BUFFET that we call...

MY DINNER WITH AMY!

Some folks believe in the RIGHT to CHOOSE…personally, I believe in the FRIGHT-TO-LIFE! This, OF CORPSE, puts ABORTION-IZING DOCTORS in a pretty INCONCEIVABLE position, especially when trying to avoid those DOOM-SAYINGLY determined FANATIC protesters! Those BABY-LOVIN' folks PLAY for keeps—no KID-ding! It's a LIFE-THREATENING, DOCTOR-STALKING, WIRE-HANGING tale of INFANTILE behavior that will have every M.D. hitting the streets HOWLING the words…

FETUS, DON'T FAIL ME NOW!

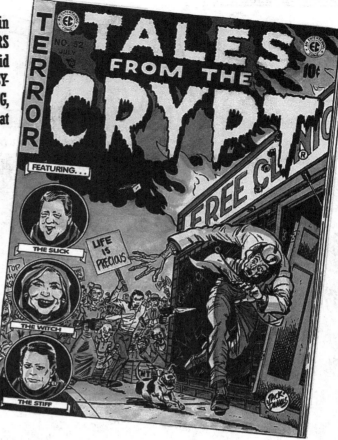

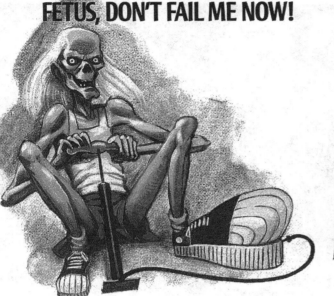

HEH! HOO! HAH! Still here, FEAR-MONGERS? Oh, you're all COLD and SHIVERY-LOOKING! Better stop all that SNEEZIN' and COFFIN, because, brother, the DOCTOR is GRIM! This is one FICKLE PHYSICIAN who will take more than your TEMPERATURE when you're feeling under the weather—SIX FEET UNDER, that is! So take two pills and call me in the MOURNING, as I prescribe the following DEADLY DOSE…

DR. KEVORKIAN'S FINAL CHECK-UP!

A MAD LOOK AT

ARTIST AND WRITER: SERGIO ARAGONES

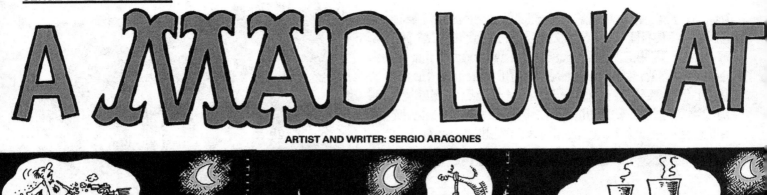

Hey, gang! It's time once again for MAD's nutty old "Cliché Monster" game. Here's how it works: Take any familiar phrase or colloquial expression, give it an eerie setting so you create a new-type monster, and you're playing it. Mainly, you're—

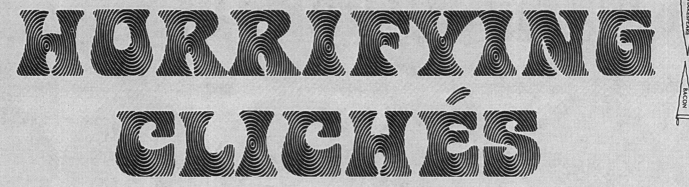

HORRIFYING CLICHÉS

ARTIST: PAUL COKER, JR.   WRITERS: PHIL HAHN & NEAL BARBERA and MAY SAKAMI

Exploding a MYTH

Dissolving a PARTNERSHIP

Re-arranging a SCHEDULE

Beating a HASTY RETREAT

Exercising a PREROGATIVE

Provoking an ARGUMENT

Curbing a VORACIOUS APPETITE

Arousing a SUSPICION

Courting a DISASTER

Tackling a TOUGH ASSIGNMENT

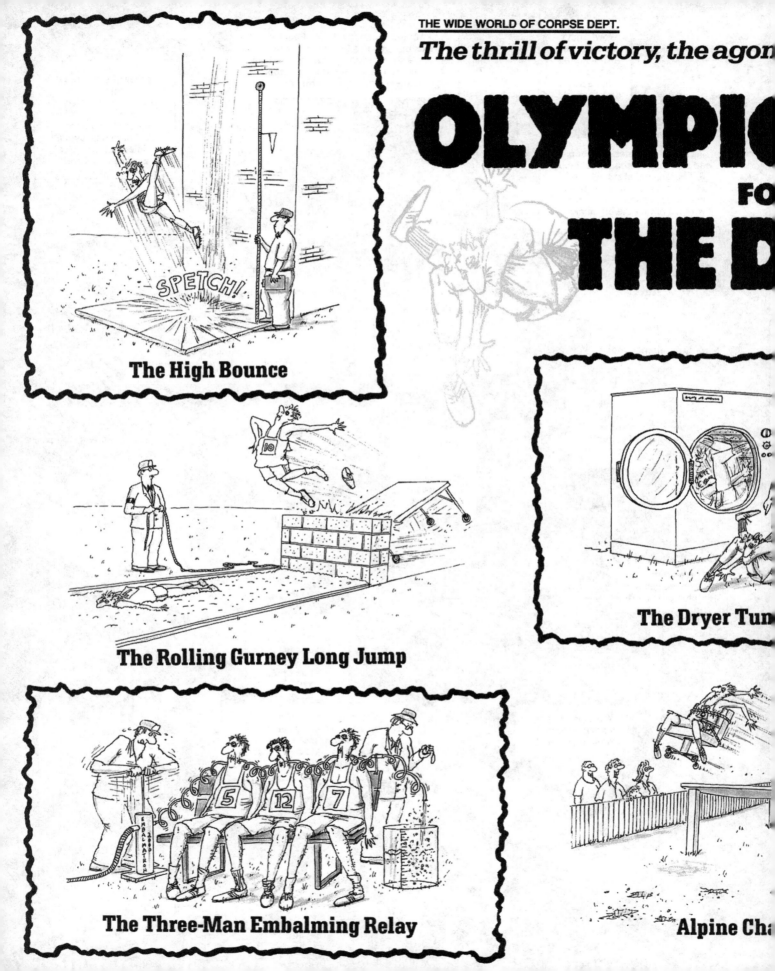

The thrill of victory, the agon

OLYMPIC

FO

THE D

The High Bounce

SPETCH!

The Rolling Gurney Long Jump

The Dryer Tun

The Three-Man Embalming Relay

Alpine Cha

It's been countless years of tortured, sleepless nights since we last played our ghoulish game! You might remember how it's played: we take a

HORRI
POLI
CLIC

ARTIST: PAUL COKER

Digging Up A SCANDAL

Twisting A FACT

Ducking A QUESTION

Reviving An OLD ISSUE

Hanging On To A SLIM LEAD

familiar phrase or expression, and interpret it our own, twisted way to create a fiendish monster! So, when better to play than election year? Here's

FYING TICAL HES

WRITER: FRANK JACOBS

The Congressman who was defeated by a hand puppet! **NEXT DONAHUE!**

Exercising A VETO

Hammering Out A COMPROMISE

Toasting A VICTORY

Breaking A PLEDGE

Launching A CAMPAIGN

Have you noticed the rash of "Horror" movies Hollywood is turning out lately? No, we're not talking about "Technicolor-Musical" Horror movies! We're talking about "B-Picture" Horror movies with monsters in them . . . monsters like "The Fly," "The Blob" and "The Creature From The Black Lagoon!" Well anyway, these Horror movies are pretty popular. And as a result, Hollywood is turning out one after another. Which is leading to a big problem: namely, the producers of these movies are running short of new ideas for monsters! So here is MAD's answer: all Hollywood has to do is take a good look at the work Madison Avenue is doing along the same lines, and their problems are solved. Then, before long, we'll all be seeing movie posters like these . . . advertising . . .

NEW from

ARTIST: WALLACE WOOD   WRITER: E. NELSON BRIDWELL

SEVEN DAYS THAT
SHOOK THE BEACH
SEE THE SPINE-TINGLING TRANSFORMATION!
FROM 97-POUND WEAKLING TO
SAND-KICKING BRUTE

THE DYNAMIC CHANGELING

PRODUCED BY:
CHARLES ATLAS

DIRECTED BY:
VIC TANNY

STARRING:

ORSON BEAN (as "The BEFORE")   VICTOR MATURE (as "The AFTER")
WITH LYLE BETTGER (as "The BARBELL") AND A HARD-PRESSED CAST

IT TORE UP THE NATION'S HIGHWAYS

THE CLUTCHING TREAD

IT STARTED IN NEW YORK AND PLOWED ITS INEXORABLE COURSE ACROSS THE COUNTRY TOWARD THE LOS ANGELES FREEWAY, DEFYING THE SPEED TRAPS, IGNORING THE ROAD SIGNS, DESTROYING ALL IN ITS PATH! THE MANIACAL INVENTION OF DOCTOR IGNATZ Q. ARMSTRONG, A DISGRUNTLED PEDESTRIAN!

LEARN THE AWFUL SECRET OF THE STRANGE BLACK DISCS
SEE THE AAA'S FUTILE ATTEMPTS TO HALT ITS PROGRESS
THRILL TO THE EXPLOSIVE CLIMAX ON A DEAD END STREET

MOVIE MONSTERS
MADISON AVENUE
500 FEET OF SLITHERING
HEXACHLOROPHINE!
The Striped Monster
From The Toothpaste Tube
See!
THE HUMAN RACE TERRORIZED BY BLOOD-CURDLING
DECAY!
See!
MANKIND'S CLOSE BRUSH WITHIN ITS
FOAMING JAWS
See!
HORROR AFTER HORROR UNTIL
THE FINAL DISSOLVE!
ONCE RELEASED, IT COULD NEVER BE RETURNED FROM WHENCE IT CAME!
MEN GASPED!
WOMEN SCREAMED!
CHILDREN WONDERED!
IT WAS THE GREATEST HORROR OF ALL TIME!
THE INCREDIBLE
LIVING
BRA
STARRING:
Selma Maidenform
Herman Questionmark
Penelope Playtex
And a firm supporting cast
"Never lets down till the final scene!"—The News
"A breathtaking and uplifting experience!"—The Mirror
"Tense . . . taut . . . gripping excitement!"—The Times

Monster movies have always been good box office when they reflected the emotional climate of their time.

When man was first learning to harness the wonders of applied science, man-made monsters were tops in popularity.

Then came the fad for overgrown species who matched the then-current emphasis on massiveness in buildings and in cities.

And with the advent of nuclear energy, horrendous new creatures were spawned by atomic explosions and radiation . . .

Now, with the world so concerned about ecology and the environment, the new wave horror films will go something like this . . .

YECCH or "What a WASTE!"

WRITER: LOU SILVERSTONE   ARTIST: DON MARTIN

A man-eating alien creature? Wow! A fight to the death between the alien and one last survivor of his rage? Hoo-boy! Such an original premise! It's already been done! This creature isn't a Predator, he's just like his...

PREDECESSOR

A nine year old boy sees ghosts everywhere he looks. That's pretty spooky! For help, he turns to a child psychologist played by Bruce Willis. That's even spookier! It shows the kid has...

THE SICK SENSE

ARTIST: ANGELO TORRES　　　**WRITER: DICK DEBARTOLO**

I'm **Doctor Malcoma Croup**, gifted **child psychologist**! As you can see by my half-hearted **smirk**, I'm particularly good at **conning childr—** er, at **TREATING** children with **psychological problems**! What a doctor **fears most** is when those children grow up to become **adults**, and realize **my treatment failed** them — as evidenced by the **semi-nude, deranged** former patient holding a **gun** on me and my **wife**! I'd offer to **help him**, but I don't accept his **HMO plan**! Tough break for him!

Remember me, Doc!? I tried to commit **suicide** by **jumping** out a third story window, **slitting** my wrists, **hanging** myself and **swallowing** poison! You classified me as "a bit **moody**," and "not very good at **completing tasks**"! Well, I **completed something** today, Doc! I found out where you **lived**, and I broke into your **home**! And I just **completed undressing**!

Please **put down** that **gun**! You're not giving my husband very much **credit** for his **outstanding work**! In all the years he's been treating people, not once did he have the **luxury** of a **totally-adjusted, well-balanced person** coming to him to seek treatment! Don't you think it wears on a **psychologist**, when only **mentally deranged** people like you — you friggin' **nutjob** — come to him for **help**!? Look, we've just **finished** an expensive **bottle** of **wine** to celebrate an **important award** my husband won! And now we're about to **make love**! So can you **put down** the **gun for 30 seconds** till he's **finished**?

I'm **Mrs. Seer**! There's something very **strange** about my son, **Cold**! Sometimes he seems to talk to **invisible people**, and when he does, the **temperature** in the house **plummets** and it gets as **cold** as a **morgue**! Sure, I wish he could be more **normal**, but on the other hand we save a **fortune** on **air conditioning**!

So that's the **new doctor** who's going to **help me**! He seems kind of **animated**! At least he seems animated when you **compare him** to the people I talk to most: **dead people**!

I'm the **family dog**! No one **walks** me or **plays** with me! And it's been **so long** since they **fed** me, I'm about to become a **dead dog**, which won't be so bad! At least once I'm **dead**, Cold will **pay more attention** to me!

Oh no! Not another movie that teams up Bruce Willis with writer/director M. Night Shyamalan! *The Sixth Sense* was bad enough! But this one is even more slow-paced, even HOKIER with its supernatural themes, even more reliant on clichéd upside-down camera angles and uses even more symbolic colors that symbolize nothing! In fact, this one is just plain...

UNBEARABLE

ARTIST: ANGELO TORRES   WRITER: DICK DEBARTOLO

This **twisted metal** is all that's left of an **express train** that left the tracks at high speed today! And THIS **lucky man** seems to be the only person still **alive!** He's actually **very lucky,** because the conductor **didn't collect** his **ticket** before the wreck, so he'll be able to **ride** for **free** on his **next trip!**

Folks, look **right into** the **camera** and tell us **who you are!**

I'm **Deadly Dull,** a security guard with so-so **psychic powers** and an even **worse fashion sense!** I mostly wear **ponchos** that hide my face! For formal affairs, I wear a **black poncho!** For the beach, I wear a **blue poncho,** and when I garden, I wear a **green poncho!** It's not like I don't have an **imagination!** My imagination is as **vast** as...er, as vast as...um, something **very, very vast!** And trust me, THAT's vast!

I was born **frail!** How frail? At the moment of **birth,** the doctor **slapped** my **butt** and broke 17 bones! The **first word** I ever uttered was "**fracture**"! Once, a guy standing next to me **blew his nose** and broke **MY neck!** The last time I **chewed** a piece of **gum,** I broke **my jaw!** I tell you, I'm **frail!**

I love my dad! I want to be **exactly like him** when I grow up! Except I **don't** want to be **bald,** I'd like to have a **wife** who **sleeps** in the **same bed** as me, I'd like to have a **decent job** and earn more than a **crappy** Security Guard's salary, I don't want to be such an **introvert,** and I look **dreadful** in a **poncho,** so I'd like to wear **ANYTHING** but one of those! Outside of that, I want to be a **carbon copy** of the **old man!**

I'm **Ordinarily Dull,** Deadly Dull's wife! Right now our **marriage** is kind of **on the rocks!** I'm not sure **exactly** what **went wrong!** We used to **love** the **same things** — attending **funerals,** staring at **blank walls,** **mumbling** over a glass of wine! But now I suspect he might be **mumbling** with **somebody else!** I've decided to give him **another chance,** because basically he's a **good man!** A **quiet man!** Almost a **dead man!**

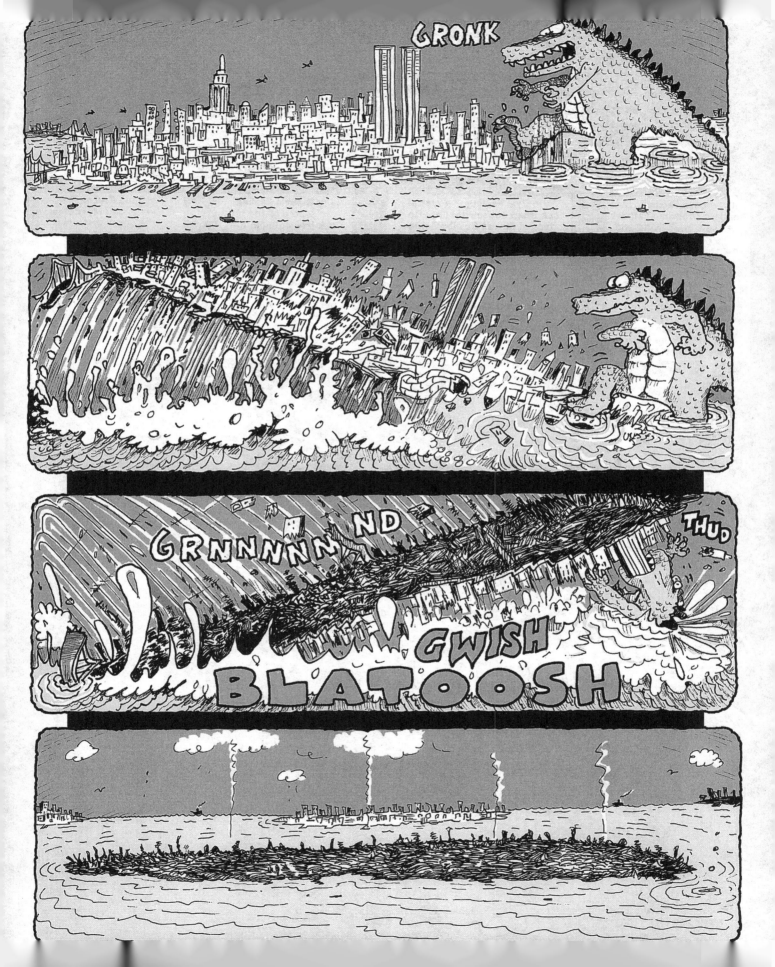

Recently, a so-called "scary" movie (by Steven Spielberg et al) made box office history when millions of horror fans all around the country rushed to theaters and paid good money to have their pants scared off them. Well, Steve and Company, MAD has taken a long, hard look at your movie, and we've come to the conclusion that using a display of dazzling special effects to cover up the lack of a strong plot and the work of unknown actors is a pretty

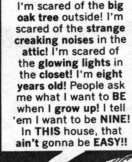

Hey, **Heave!!** Something's **wacko** with your **TV!**

Yeah! We're trying to watch the **foot-ball game,** and the **channel selector** keeps **switching** to some **dopey KIDDIE SHOW!!**

Oh…that's my **neighbor's remote control unit!** It has a **strange effect** on **MY set!** What's the **score,** anyway…?

I don't know, but I think the **Rams** just tackled Kermit, the Frog!!

What are we **doing, Mommy?**

Burying your **pet canary** that **died!**

But it's such a **teensie weensie little plot!!**

Don't worry! **Lots** of people manage to do **very well** with just such a teensie weensie little plot!

Really…? Like **WHO,** Mommy??

Like Steven **Spielberg,** the **creator** of **this film!**

ARTIST: JACK DAVIS   WRITER: ARNIE KOGEN

What's troubling you **now,** Blobbie?

Everything! It's the **thunder** and the **lightning** and the **ominous clouds** and that **big weird gnarled old tree!**

A **big brave eight-year-old** like **you?!** You're **not worried** about it, **are** you?

Let me put it **this way:** Living in **this house** is giving me an "**ulcerette**"!

I guess that stuff can be **pretty scary** to a kid! It's **natural** to want to **cry,** or **hide under the covers!** But when you **grow up,** Son, you'll find yourself coping with problems in a **more adult way!**

—PUFF—
—PUFF—
So **how** was your **day,** Hon?
—PUFF—

Don't ask!! But—PUFF—PUFF—it's **getting better** every second!!

BLOBBIE!! What are you **LOOKING** at…?!

Mom and **Dad** …coping with their problems in a more "adult way"!

In the mid-nineteenth century, Poet Edgar Allen Poe made people scream in horror with his masterpiece poem *The Raven*! One hundred fifty years later, MAD Magazine gets much the same result when it publishes its poem about *Scream* filmmaker...

Wes Craven

with apologies to Edgar Allen Poe

Once upon a midnight dreary, horror flicks did not seem weary,
"Elm Street," "Halloween," and "Friday...the 13th" scared fans galore.
Michael, Jason and that Freddie, made fan's stomachs feel unsteady,
But no one was really ready, for schlock sequels by the score.
Which director was most guilty of these schlock clones by the score?
    'Twas Wes Craven, king of gore.

Soon this genre was outdated, fans no longer were elated,
By the bloodbaths that these movies seemed to churn out more and more.
But one day an unknown writer, wrote a chiller that seemed brighter,
Craven helmed this newest frighter, which made fun of flicks of yore.
Why would Craven want to mock his horror films from days of yore?
    'Cause Wes Craven was a whore!

Would his "Scream" become a winner, forcing fans to lose their dinner?
It seemed doubtful since its only star was young Drew Barrymore.
Drew had peaked when she was seven, and got drunk by age eleven,
So how in the name of heaven would this film get off the floor?
Very soon it mattered not when Drew's guts splattered on the floor.
    On her, Craven slammed the door.

ARTIST: BILL WRAY   WRITER: ANDREW J. SCHWARTZBERG

Wes Craven

E very horror fan was shaken, when Drew's life was quickly taken,
If this movie's biggest star was killed what else might be in store?
Was Neve Campbell next to buy it? Many hoped that Wes would try it,
For no fright fan could deny it — Neve was such a whiny bore.
Could a movie be successful with a whining, pouting bore?
 "Yes!" Wes Craven's fans did roar.

T his flick flew not on its story, or the fact that it was gory,
This film thrived upon the fact that it made "in-jokes" by the score.
Making fun of Tori Spelling, Fonzie at the students yelling,
One lone film geek always telling what we should be frightened for.
When he saw this Gen-X chiller was what fans were waiting for,
 Quoth Wes Craven, "Let's make more."

A h, distinctly all remember, one year later in December,
"Scream 2" was released upon the public with a mighty roar.
This plot had a large infusion of dumb twists that caused confusion.
What bizarre drug-crazed delusion, made this script a muddled bore?
Laurie Metcalf as the killer — could there be a bigger bore?
 Still, cash Craven made galore.

"*S*cream" flicks sure were money makers, so it spawned a pack of fakers.
"I Know What You Did Last Summer" was the first to wash ashore.
"Urban Legend," "Mrs. Tingle," these and more all seemed to mingle,
Each and every freakin' single of these flicks we did abhor.
Who began this competition of scare flicks we did abhor?
　　　'Twas Wes Craven launched this war.

*N*ext, two years of hype and rumors, growing like malignant tumors,
Built "Scream 3" up in a way that no one living could ignore.
Once again Neve acted schmucky, in a sequel that was sucky,
Worse, in fact, than "Bride of Chucky," was this flick that was a bore.
The killer was — well, we won't tell you, should you plan to see this bore.
　　　Just blame Craven when you snore.

*N*ow Wes Craven's "Screams" are staying, always playing, always playing,
In the VCRs and theaters frequented by teens galore.
And they say "3" is the last one, but we think they'll pull a fast one,
We bet they've begun to cast one, for there's money in this gore.
Yes we're sure we'll see another pointless film with pointless gore,
　　　When Wes Craven makes "Scream 4."

PECK'S BAD BOY DEPT.

The Devil means big business for the movie industry these days. First came "Rosemary's Baby"... then "The Exorcist" ... and now, this latest film. It's apparent movie fans go for

THE O

MENOUS

How old is the baby today?

He's three panels old!

Three panels?!

That's the way we show the passage of time in a magazine!

Look! The maid just jumped out the window and HUNG HERSELF!

Aren't you upset about this, Mr. Ambassador?

Not really! After all, she did it on her own time! This IS her lunch hour!

ARTIST: HARRY NORTH, ESQ. WRITER: DICK DE BARTOLO

I must talk to you about a most urgent matter!

I gave at the office!

In that case, I gave at home!

But this IS your office!

Listen to what I have to say, Mr. Ambassador! You are in serious trouble! You must turn to HIM above! You must drink His blood and eat His body!

Too late! I just had a frankfurter and an orange!

You don't understand! Your son is Satan . . . Lucifer . . . Beelzebub . . . Mephistopheles . . . The Demon of Darkness!

Now that you mention it . . . he HAS been acting like a little DEVIL lately . . . !

Ah-HAH!! Then you BELIEVE ME?!?

I believe your collar may be on a little too tight! Kids can't be angels all the time!

ENDING ON A SOUR NOTE

ARTIST: GEORGE WOODBRIDGE

A MAD LOOK AT

ARTIST AND WRITER:
SERGIO ARAGONES

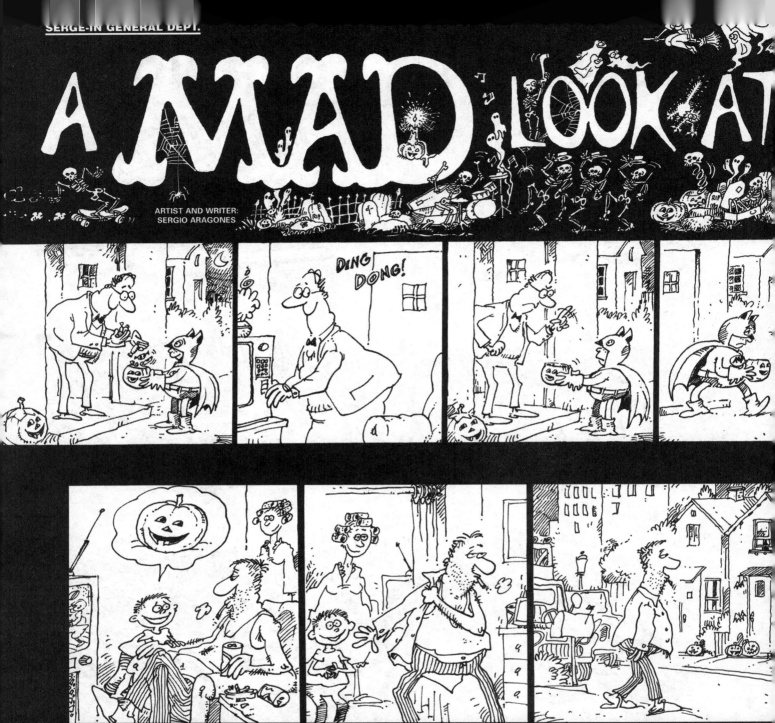

R.L. Stine's series of Goosebumps books is supposed to scare kids with tales of werewolves and monsters. These things aren't very scary, however, when compared to a youngster's real life! Perhaps Mr. Stine should write some stories that are truly terrifying, like these...

GOOSEBUMPS HORROR STORIES THAT WOULD REALLY SCARE KIDS

R.L. STINE

Goosebumps

THE HORROR HAND-ME-DOWNS

SCHOOLSPASTIC

R.L. STINE

Goosebumps

ATTACK OF THE PINCHING GRANDMA

SCHOOLSPASTIC

ARTIST: JOE ORLANDO   WRITER: DARREN JOHNSON

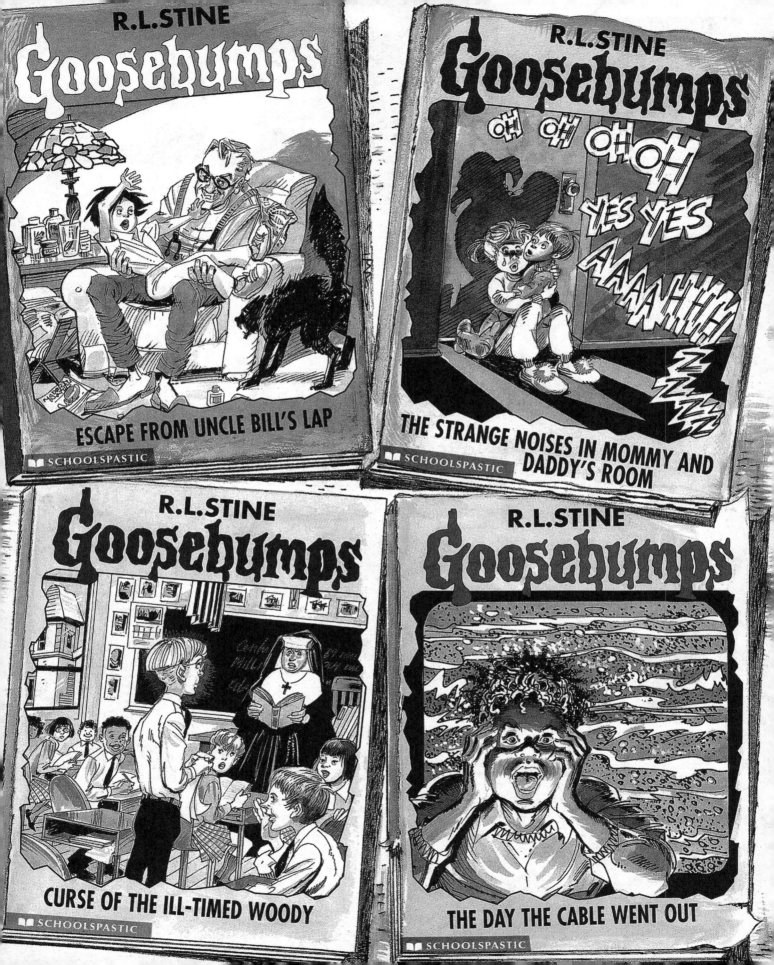

SCREE
I'm Wes Raving-Looney, the horror film director and splatter master! You all know my trademark — a nut in a ghost mask, a knife, and a conveniently-placed co-ed! My early films were basically standard slasher fare, traditional blood and violence! And they did okay. But I recently discovered a commercial gold mine! I've combined the typical gore with hip irreverence! Some tongue-in-cheek, some knife-in-liver...It's a formula that's delighted the critics and, more importantly, thrilled my accountants!
The genre is known as "Horror-Comedy"! I love horror. I love comedy. I'll give you an example: In any one of my films, what do you call it when 43 teenage babes have been killed? Tuesday! Get it? You see, on Wednesday there's...ah, I'll let MAD do the bad jokes in their version of my recent hit horror spoof...
Have you ever noticed there are never any African-American characters or victims in these slasher films?
I have a feeling that in this movie we're about to have racially-balanced carnage! Our people are making progress!
POST MORTEM MOVIE MAKES A KILLING...
I'm the richest man in the community!
What do you do? Computers? Real Estate?
Nah! Too risky! I own the store that sells ghost masks and robes!
Wow! Bill Gates move over!
Hey, Tiffany, could you lend me $100?
What for?
I want to look cool for the sorority party! I'm getting my ears, tongue and navel pierced!
Save your money! Hang around this town long enough, eventually you'll have your whole body pierced for free!
Excuse me, we're here to see Flubber!
Man, do YOU have the wrong theater!
torres

Don Martin proved Darwin's theory in reverse, 'cause they certainly made a monkey out of him when he tried impressing the natives there as

THE GOOD DOCTOR IN AFRICA

For the Sportsman

○ "Tarheel State" ○
10-S-NE-1
N. CAROLINA '61

A few years back (MAD #53), we noted how Hollywood was scraping the bottom of the barrel trying to dig up new and scarier movie monsters for their horror pictures — monsters like "The Fly", "The Blob", "The Creature From The Black Lagoon" and "Nick Adams". We then suggested that Hollywood take a good look at the monsters being created by Madison Avenue for their inspiration. Now, we add more fool to the fire by suggesting these . . .

NEW FROM

H.P. LOVECRAFT

WHAT INDESCRIBABLE HORRORS LURKED IN THE BOX THAT MADE STRONG MEN TREMBLE, WOMEN FAINT AND CHILDREN SCREAM?

YOU'LL **SHRIEK** IN **TERROR**
at the bills

YOU'LL **SHUDDER** WITH **NAUSEA**
at the junk mail

YOU'LL **GASP** IN **SURPRISE**
at a real letter

THINGS
IN THE
MAILBOX

STARRING

TOM **POSTAGE**   FRED **ASTAMP**   MARTY **MAILER**   RIP **TORN**

and introducing OCCUPANT as "The Victim"

BEWARE!

LOCK THE DOORS!   DRAW THE BLINDS!   TURN OUT THE LIGHTS!

The Neighbors Are Coming!

SEE THEM
produce snapshots
by the hundreds!

HEAR THEM
talk and talk for
hours about nothing!

WATCH THEM
eat every drop of
food in sight!

AS THEY STAY AND STAY AND STAY!

THEY CAME FROM DOWN THE BLOCK

THE MANHATTAN MONSTER MONKEYSHINE

ARTIST AND WRITER: DUCK EDWING

THE NEARSIGHTED VOODOO PRIEST

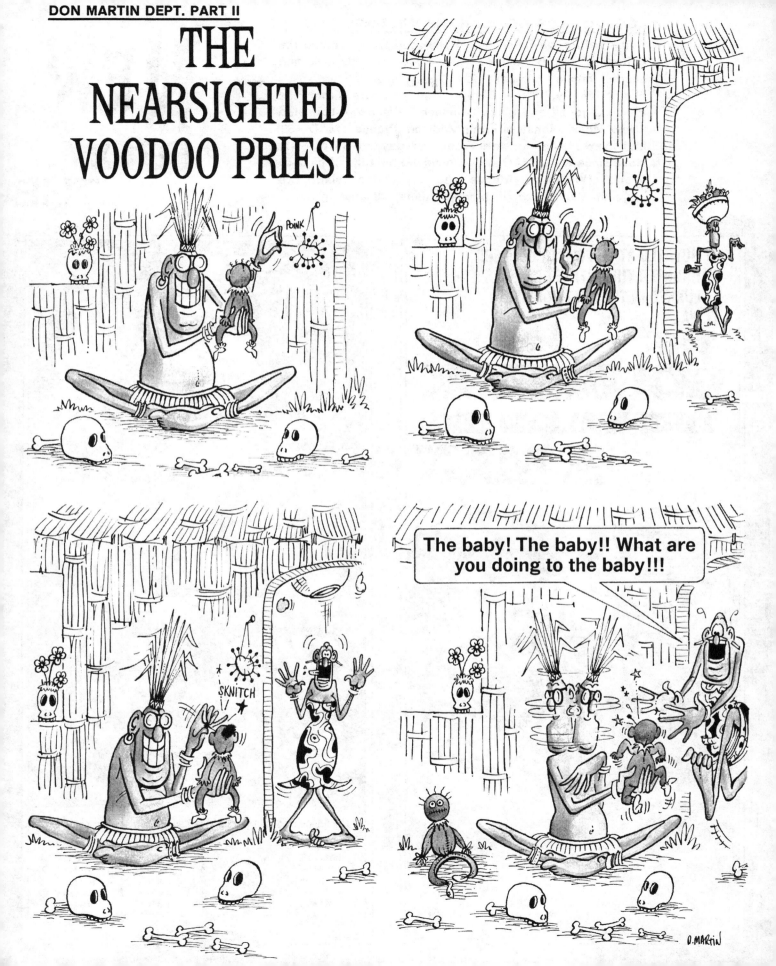

I GOT MY BLOB THROUGH THE N.Y. TIMES DEPT.

Twice before we noted how Hollywood was scraping the bottom of the barrel trying to come up with new and scarier movie monsters for their horror pictures . . . like "The Fly," "The Blob," "The Creature From The Black Lagoon" and "Troy Donahue." We then suggested "New Movie Monsters From Madison Avenue" (MAD #53) and "New Movie Monsters From Everyday Life" (MAD #81). Now, since we at MAD know so much about the "Business World" (We've got friends who work for a living!), we suggest the following blood-curdling, disgusting . . . . .

NEW FROM THE

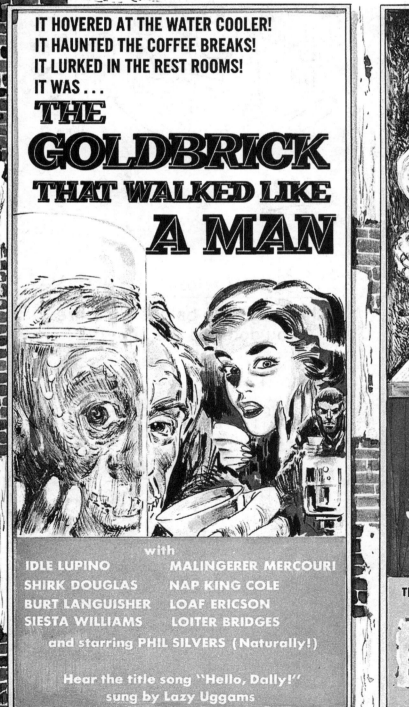

MOVIE MONSTERS

BUSINESS WORLD

ARTIST: JOE ORLANDO   WRITER: E. NELSON BRIDWELL

WHEN HE OPENED HIS MOUTH, OUT CAME
IDIOCY   BALONEY   HOT AIR
YET NO ONE DARED MOVE! THEY JUST HAD TO
STAND THERE AND SUFFER, LISTENING TO . . .

THE AMAZING COLOSSAL BORE

. . . BECAUSE HE WAS TOO BIG TO STOP!
MAINLY BECAUSE HE WAS ALSO "THE BOSS"!

HEAR SAM SAY:
"That's great, J.B.!"

HEAR CLYDE SAY:
"That's rich, J.B.!"

HEAR IRVING SAY:
"That's a good one, J.B.!"

HEAR ALFRED SAY:
"That's enough! I quit, J.B.!"

Written By	Directed By	Produced By	Edited By	Music By	Arranged By	Photography By	Narrated By
HUGH DOWNS	DURWOOD KIRBY	ARTHUR GODFREY	BENNETT CERF	LAWRENCE WELK	OZZIE NELSON	ALLEN FUNT	ED REIMERS

WITH THEIR PALMS OUTSTRETCHED, THEY KEPT COMING . . . AND COMING . . .
THERE WAS NO PLACE TO HIDE! THERE WAS NO ESCAPE FROM . . .

THE CREATURES with the OFFICE COLLECTIONS

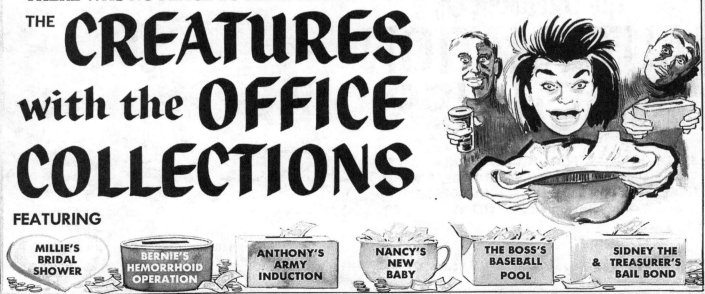

FEATURING

MILLIE'S BRIDAL SHOWER

BERNIE'S HEMORRHOID OPERATION

ANTHONY'S ARMY INDUCTION

NANCY'S NEW BABY

THE BOSS'S BASEBALL POOL

SIDNEY THE & TREASURER'S BAIL BOND

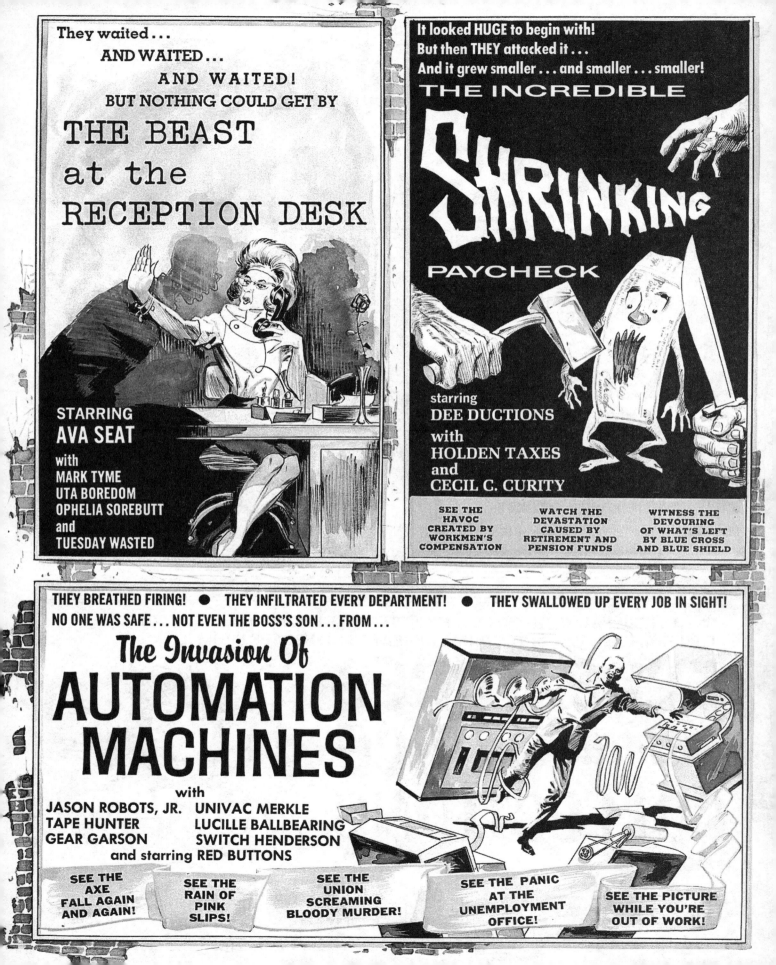

Recently, we gave four blank pages to two idiots. They planned to use the four pages to create a hysterically funny movie parody.

However, things did not go as planned. This is all that remains.

THE BLAND WITCH PROJECT

I'm **Heifer!** I want to **escape** the **woods**, and I want to somehow **survive** this **horror!** But what I really want is to **direct!** I have a **vision!** So what if that vision is **blurry** and **shakes** all over the place? As you'll see, I like to film the **exact same stuff** over again and again — so I'm already as **good** a director as **Spike Lee!** The **only trouble** is, what happens to me in this movie is the **ULTIMATE** one-picture deal! Forget about any **sequels!**

I'm **Squash,** and I came here to answer a **mysterious question!** And no, that question is **NOT** "Hey, aren't you the guy who used to be in the **Spin Doctors?**" A lot of things that **happen** in this movie **get me angry!** But what **pisses me off** most of all is something that doesn't happen! I'm the only **long-haired dude** in the history of horror movies who **DOESN'T get laid moments** before he **gets killed!**

I'm **Meatball!** I wear a **snug, form-fitting outfit** throughout the movie! Unfortunately, it's a **poncho!** I'm the voice of **reason** who raises some **troubling issues** about this whole **project!** However, I wait until we're in the **middle** of a freakin' **forest** to raise those issues! Okay, so my **timing's a tad off!** When we get back to **civilization,** I **might** buy some Microsoft stock — I have a **feeling** it could be **worth something** someday!

I'm **Heifer again!** Since there's only a grand total of **three characters** in this **whole damn movie,** it's tough for MAD to **fill out** this **intro panel!** So, how do you like this **caricature** of me from a **different angle?** Neat, huh?

Hi, I'm **Myluck** and this is **Saycheez!** We're the **directors** of this "**documentary**"! We sent our actors into the woods **without a script,** and made them do all the **filming work!** To create the **realistic feel** of this movie, we made our actors **sleep** in **dirt,** fall into **cold water, eat buggy food,** go **without sleep** and freeze their **asses off!** We originally got the idea while we were **head counselors** at summer camp!

Hi, I'm **Calista Flockhart!** I came to learn some **diet tips** from those spooky **wooden stick men** that are all over the forest! I'm so **envious** of them! No matter how **carefully** I eat, I just can't get below a **12-inch waist!**

ARTIST: BILL WRAY   WRITER: DESMOND DEVLIN

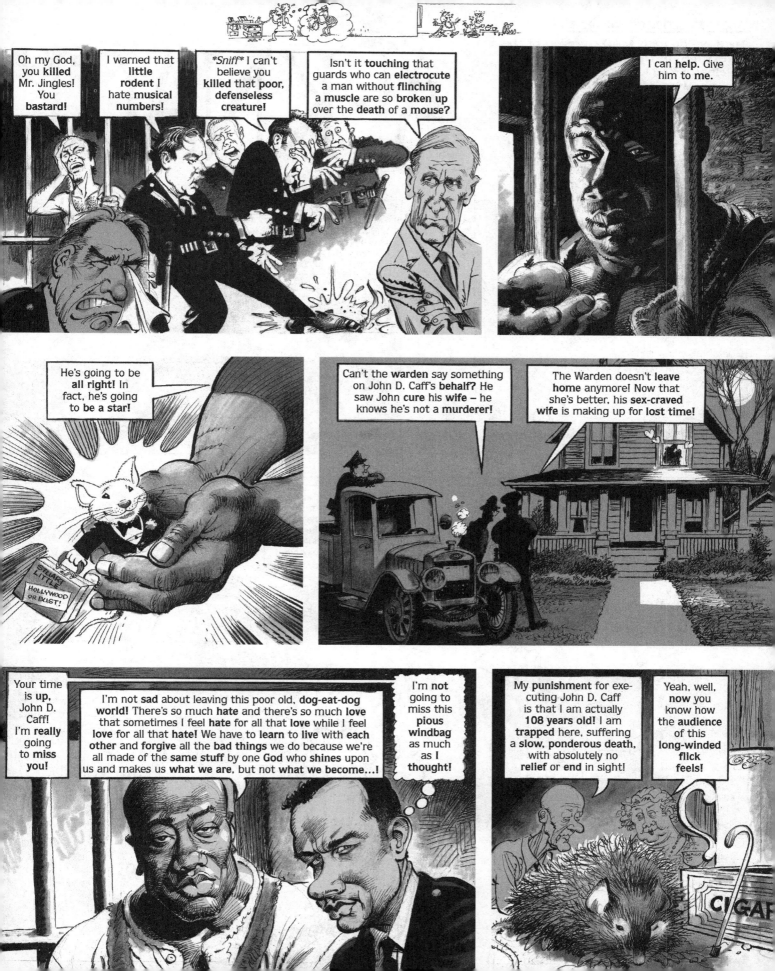

A·KNACK

ARTIST: PAUL COKER

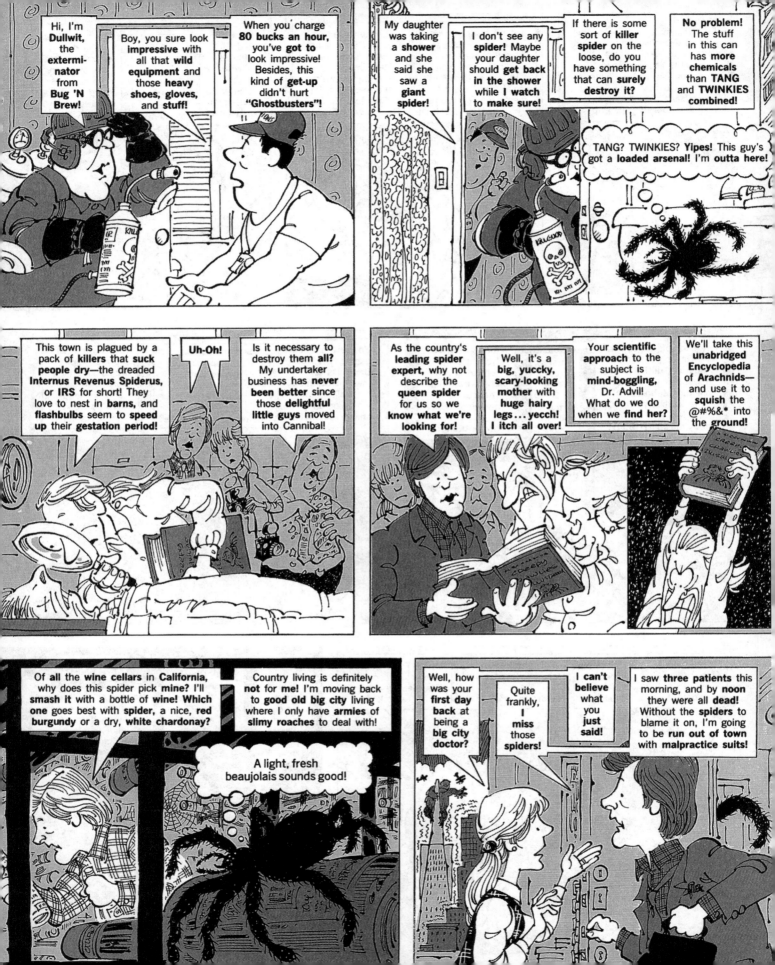

There is one group we at MAD can't tolerate – whiners! From politicians complaining about negative ads to dot-com sock puppets who can't take a joke to the biggest whiner of them all, Kathie Lee Gifford – we hate 'em, we hate 'em, WE HATE 'EM! Having said that, we must admit that there are certain people with justifiable beefs. The chronically ill, the elderly, and of course, homicidal maniacs! It's time for...

LEGITIMATE GRIPES
OF YOUR
AVERAGE
SERIAL KILLER

FWAT
FWAT
FWAT!

GUESS WHO'S GAY??

The actress you've hacked your way through nine states to impress suddenly comes out of the closet.

While digging a shallow grave in the backyard for your latest victim, you accidentally hit the cable TV line.

ARTIST AND WRITER: JOHN CALDWELL

LEGITIMATE GRIPES
OF YOUR
AVERAGE
SERIAL KILLER

You're watching *America's Most Wanted*'s re-enactment of your latest caper and not only is the woman playing the hooker someone you wouldn't be caught dead bludgeoning, but the guy playing you can't act his way out of a plastic trash bag.

So-called "freezer proof" stickers that aren't.

Telemarketers who always call during meals.

You put up Manson-like numbers in a two-year nationwide reign of terror, but give yourself one homemade tattoo in the mirror and suddenly you're the laughing stock of death row.

It's hard to wreak "chainsaw" terror if you're on a "Sears Craftsman Jigsaw" budget.

When you think: Would it kill your mother to let ONE appliance guy finish fixing the dryer before ordering you to dispose of him?

You run out of blood before you can finish your cryptic evil message on the bathroom mirror.

Your doctor orders you to cut out red ...t immediately and there you sit with

Sure, where were all the marriage proposals from attractive single women who don't mind that your hobbies include carving down-on-their-luck drifters into duck decoys *before* you got caught?

Hey, gang! It's time once again for MAD's nutty old "Cliché Monster" game. Here's how it works: Take any familiar phrase or colloquial expression, give it an eerie setting so you create a new-type monster, and you're playing it. Mainly, you're—

HORRIFYING CLICHÉS

ARTIST: PAUL COKER, JR.   WRITERS: MAY SAKAMI & E. NELSON BRIDWELL

Leaning heavily on an EXPERIENCE

Shouldering a RESPONSIBILITY

Making a LONG STORY short

Striking a CARELESS POSE

Cementing a RELATIONSHIP

Creating a DISTURBANCE

Wrestling with a WEIGHTY PROBLEM

Carried away by an ENTHUSIASM

Raising a RUCKUS

Splitting an INFINITIVE

Ironing out a DIFFICULTY

Getting out of a TIGHT SQUEEZE

Launching a CAREER

Mounting an OFFENSIVE

Releasing one's INHIBITIONS

Killing off a few IDLE HOURS

Scenes We'd Like to See

The Monster and the Villagers

Are you paranoid? Do you think your so-called friends and family want nothing more than to ruin your life? To fill it with misery and suffering? Well calm down, Spazzo, 'cause we here at MAD are happy to put your fears to rest. Your loved ones aren't out to get you! But someone else is...

KNOW YOUR

SHAQUESHA

Causes water to splash onto your crotch, so it looks like you have the bladder control of your 97-year-old grandfather

LUMPY

Cranks up the volume on your radio, so when you start you car in the morning you're suddenly blasted into oblivion by teeth-rattling, brain-piercing, eardrum-damaging music

LAQUITA

Pushes all your sheets to the bottom of the bed, so you wake up colder than Leonardo DiCaprio's frozen lifeless corpse at the end of *Titanic*

FRANZ

BARTLETT

Trips you in front of a crowd of at least 45 people, so you look like a freakin' spazoid

Makes your grandmother walk in on you while you're watching a movie with your date at the precise moment a sex scene starts

GHOSTS

ARTIST: JAMES WARHOLA

WRITER: RYAN PAGELOW

LAPPY

Enjoys tormenting you by playing The "Hide-Your-Only-Working-Pen-in-the-Drawer-Full-of-Dozens-of-Dried-Up-Totally-Useless-Pens" game

RUPUS

Makes any shirt that looks good on you itch as if your entire back was being attacked by flesh-eating fire ants

JO-JO

Puts bags of repulsive barbecue popcorn that no one ever buys in front of the chips you love in the vending machine

BUMPTON

Makes the shower either skin-numbing freezing cold or skin-disintegrating scalding hot no matter how you adjust the shower knob

MURRAY

Wakes you up at the wildest part of your deviant sex dream and prevents you from returning to it when you go back to sleep

Want to see a feel-good movie with shiny, happy characters and an uplifting storyline that will have you leaving the theater in high spirits, happy to be alive, with a smile on your face and a song in your heart? Then stay away from...

THE

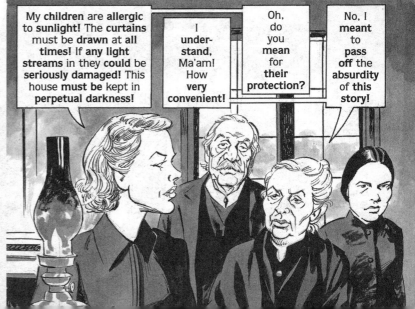

GOTSILLY

ARTIST: ANGELO TORRES   WRITER: DICK DEBARTOLO

We **brought** you here to **see** these **gigantic footprints**, doctor! Any **thoughts?**

Yeah, if **Dr. Scholl** could sell the **guy** who made these **prints** just **one pair** of **insoles**, he could **retire!** Man, what **large feet!** He must use a **hedge trimmer** to cut his **toe nails!**

I **told** the Colonel this **wasn't** your **field**, Dr. Tattoo! I'm **Elsea**, the hot-to-trot **paleontologist!** Does your **wife work** with you?

No, I'm **single!**

No girl-friend!

Nineties or not, there's definitely **no boy-friend!**

Elsea, **suppose** we **work** on **stalking** what made these **footprints first!** You can **work** on **stalking** Dr. Tattoo **after hours!**

Great! Do you have a **girlfriend?**

Boy-friend? This is the **'90s...**

This **foot-age** was just **released** by the **French!**

It's **typical** of French Cinema! **Pretentious, no plot, terrible directing, bad special effects!**

This is **news footage,** Doctor! It **shows** a Japanese **ship** that was **attacked** yesterday! It's the **second** ship to **sink mysteriously** in **two days!**

Sometimes those overzealous **Greenpeace** volunteers get **a little carried away!**

I **believe** the **giant footprints** have **something** to do with **these ships!**

This **may not** be my **field** of **expertise**, but **ships do not** make **footprints!**

Hmmm, he's **right** about **that!** But look at this **map** — the **X's** mark all the **boats** that have **recently sunk!**

And **what** do you **think** these **hearts** indicate?

Nude beaches! I put those on the **map!**

THE WEREWOLF

ARTIST: GEORGE WOODBRIDGE   WRITER: SEMI

MEDI-SCARE DEPT.

Hey, gang! Here we go again in our never-ending quest for new inspirations for Hollywood

NEW MOVIE MONSTERS

THEY CAME BY DAY . . . THEY CAME BY NIGHT . . .
DRAWING THE BLOOD FROM THEIR VICTIM'S VEINS!

*And when it came time to operate, they
put it all back . . . and charged for it!*

"THE BLOOD-TEST VAMPIRES"

SEE THE UNSPEAKABLE BLOBS THAT
MADE WOMEN FAINT AT THEIR SIGHT
AND STRONG MEN'S STOMACHS TURN!

"THE HORRORS OF THE HOSPITAL DIET"

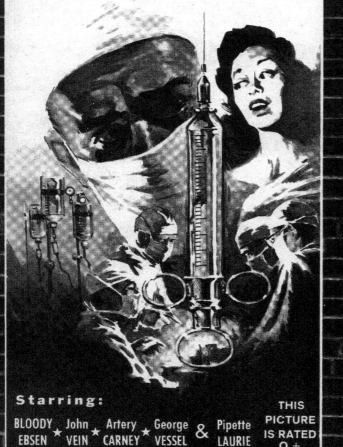

Starring:

BLOODY EBSEN ★ John VEIN ★ Artery CARNEY ★ George VESSEL & Pipette LAURIE

THIS PICTURE IS RATED O +

STARRING:

Elisha COOK with Stew GRANGER ★ Steam McQUEEN ★ Broil IVES ★ David FRY & Milton BOIL

WHAT WAS
THE HORRIBLE
ICY TOUCH
THAT CHILLED
MEN'S HEARTS?

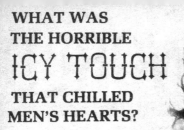

It was the
Stethoscope...in

"THE ORDEAL OF THE CHECK-UP"

WITH

Tapper KNEE ★ Prober GROIN ★ Poker GUTT ★ Phil D. GLANZ & Luke N. DeMOUTH

HE RANG AND RANG AND RANG! HE CRIED OUT TIME AND TIME AND TIME AGAIN! BUT NO ONE CAME! WHAT WAS THE AWFUL ANSWER TO . . .

"THE MYSTERY OF THE VANISHING NURSE"

WHAT WERE THESE STRANGE CONCOCTIONS? WHY DID THEY TASTE SO TERRIBLE . . . AND COST SO MUCH?
THEY WERE MEDICINES THAT GREW AND MULTIPLIED IN THE BATHROOM CABINET UNTIL THEY BECAME . . .

"THE THINGS IN THE BOTTLES"

THIS
PICTURE
IS RATED
X
sedrin

STARRING:

PENNY SILLIN ★ TERRY MYSIN ★ AL K. SELTZER ★ DONNA GEL ★ LIZ TUREEN ★ ANNA SINN ★ KAY O'PECTATE ★ ABE ZORBEEN, JR. ★ SARAH TAN ★ JERRY TOLL ★ ROBERT TUSSIN ★ MEG NESIA & CORA SYDIN as Auntie Histamine

A BOY
and his
CHEMISTRY
SET

Tom Cruise is a vampire. A 12-year old unknown actress is a vampire. Brad Pitt and Antonio Banderas are vampires. What else can we say about it all, except — he sucks, she sucks, they suck and so does...

INTRAVENOUS WITH THE

A Witch's Tale

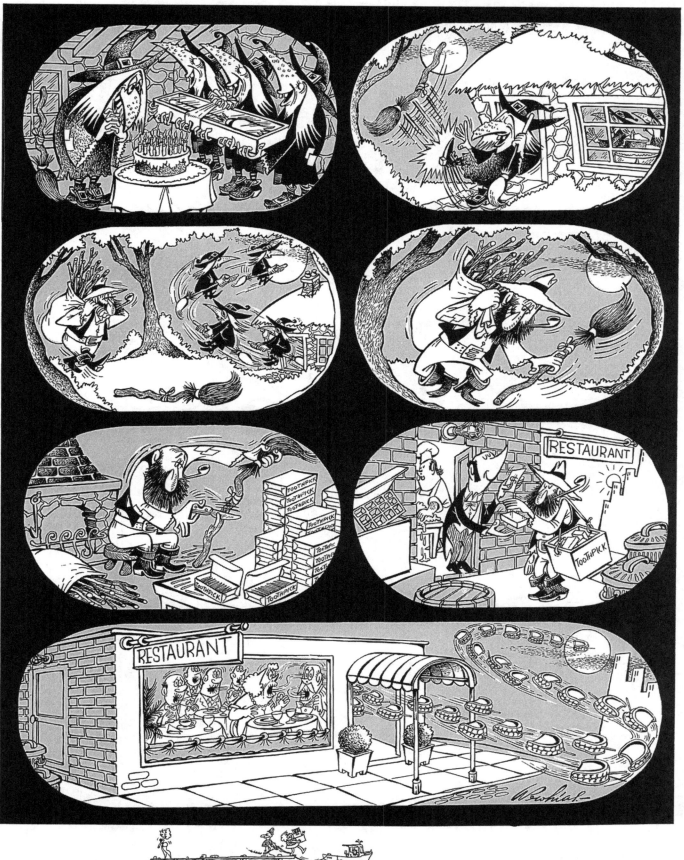

HALLOWEEN

WRITER: JEFF KRUSE

ARTIST: PETER BAGGE

4 Having to share your candy with a younger sibling who didn't do any of the work.

5 The fact that candy companies have the gall to create the phrase "Fun Size" when what they really mean is "Extremely Small Size."

6 Glow-in-the-dark cardboard skeletons that don't even try to accurately recreate the ulna.

10 Finding an empty candy bowl on a porch, because the owners counted on the honor system and you got there second.

TAKE ONE

11 The humiliating — not to mention idiotic — party tradition of bobbing for apples. Just what we want to do — dip our faces in a simmering broth of other kids' sweat, drool and pinkeye bacteria!

12 Trying to play kickball at recess in a bulky costume.

YOW!

A new film recently debuted which stars a legendary monster portrayed by a Hollywood leading man. Opening to rave reviews and big business at the box office, the film is long on gorey, bloody scenes juxtaposed against tender moments of love and human tragedy. Yeah, we can't wait to see Interview With the Vampire! We might even spoof it next issue! For now, here's our spoof of...

FRANKENSLIME

I am **Vicgore Frankenslime!** If I **have** my **way**, a **mother** will **never** again **die** during **child birth**, like mine did! My **controversial** plan calls for making the **fathers pregnant!** I **also** believe I can **bring** people **back** from the **dead** — which is **good news** for my **patients** since I'm a **totally incompetent doctor!**

Pay **no** attention to that fool **Frankenslime!** He **still** studies the **ravings** of **ancient medical lunatics!** Here at the **University of Indigent Medicine,** I **teach** my students the ways of **modern medical lunatics!**

I'm **Professor Wildman!** I've **abandoned** my **attempts** to **bring** people **back** from the **dead!** My **experiments** had **terrible consequences** for **mankind!** Actually, I'm **still trying** to bring **one patient back** to life who died without paying a **large medical bill** — but **only** so he can **settle** the **account!** Then I'll **quit** the **business** for **good!**

I am **Hernia, Vicgore's fellow** medical **student!** I'm **not** as **advanced** as **him** in my **medical undertakings!** He's trying to **retrieve** people **back** from the **dead!** Me, I'm still trying to **retrieve** my **lab coat** back from the **laundry!**

I'm **Lizbit,** an orphan raised by the **Frankenslime** family! **Vicgore** and I were **raised** like **brother** and **sister!** His **father** gave me **advice** like a **Dutch Uncle!** Now, **Vicgore** and I are like **kissing cousins,** unless we're **fighting,** then we're more like **husband** and **wife!** Frankly, I'm **sick** of **relatives** already, which is **rare** for an **orphan!**

ARE YOU TALKING TO ME?

BARF BAG

COURTESY OF SWISSAIR

ARTIST: ANGELO TORRES   WRITER: DICK DEBARTOLO

Nowhere are the successes of the women's movement more evident than on television. From the leather-clad, butchy Xena to the non-leather clad, butchy Ellen, women are braving new worlds, breaking new ground and forging new relationships! The latest breakthrough is a non-butchy (most definitely), non-leather-clad (unfortunately), hot little high school student in short, short skirts whose hobby is hunting down and killing the undead! You might know her as...

Busty the vampire spayer

ARTIST: ANGELO TORRES   WRITER: DICK DeBARTOLO

I'm **Pillow!** It **amazes** me that **no one catches on** to what **really** goes on in this **library!** Look at the **shelves** — **two books** on math, **two books** on **history, two books** on **geography** and **11,000 books** on **vampires, witchcraft,** and **devil worship!** I have a **crush** on **Extender,** but he has a **crush** on **Busty!** So what do I do for **dates?** Being a **computer nerd,** I turn to **AOL** for **help!** But I **never** seem to **find** anybody who **responds** to me in my **chatroom:** "Plain, Uninteresting, Mousy, Unattractive Girl Seeks Hunk"! Maybe it'd work if **changed** "Hunk" to "Dream Guy"!

I'm **HardCordella!** I'm **beautiful,** I'm **rich,** I'm **sexy,** and I'm **very popular** with the **boys,** because I'm also **easy!** Some of the girls here think I'm a **"witch"** or a **"bitch"!** Actually, I'm **both! Whatever!** Despite their **jealousy,** the girls have voted me **Most Likely Target For A Hit And Run Accident!** Hey, I'm **well-liked!** What can I **say?**

I'm **Angle,** a **good vampire!** A **good vampire** is a **tortured soul** who wants to **do good,** but **sometimes** just **slips into evil!** You know, like **Clinton** and **Gore** and their **fundraising practices!** Busty and I have the **hots** for **each other,** but she's **afraid** to go on a **date** with me! Hundreds of years of **bad press** about the way us **vampires kiss** is hard to **overcome!**

BEWARE
LIBRARY CLOSES AT DUSK
FOR OBVIOUS REASONS

HORNY LITTLE DEVIL

RENFIELD HALL

TRANSYLVANIA STATION

666

RIP TORN

RIP TAYLOR

A cup of **bat lips**... the skin of a **boa constrictor**... the blood of a **newt**... eye of **toad**...

Very **impressive!** Are you the **chemistry teacher?**

No, I'm the **cafeteria cook!**

What did you guys do in **biology class** today?

The **usual** — **dissected** and **buried** another **body** with a **stake** through its **heart!** The teacher said they make **great fertilizer!** But we bury so **many,** the **plants** on **campus** are **growing** by **leaps** and **bounds,** and disturbing the **ecological balance!**

I made the **tombstone** you used in **arts** and **crafts** today! That's **all** we've done lately — ceramic **projects!** We make **tombstones** for graves, **urns** for ashes...how is this **preparing me** for my **SATs?**

ONE-ON-ONE NIGHT IN THE LABORATORY

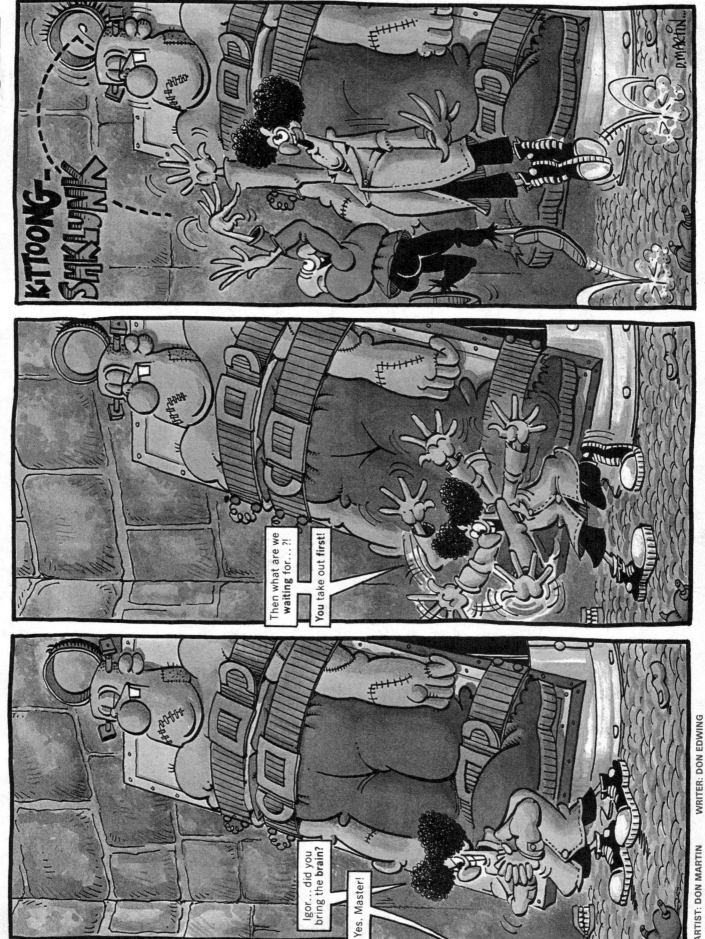

ARTIST: DON MARTIN   WRITER: DON EDWING

A MAD LOOK AT THE

ARTIST AND WRITER: SERGIO ARAGONES

MUMMY RETURNS

MR. FIX-IT

Tackles your Occult and Paranormal Home Repair Problems

ARTIST: JAMES WARHOLA   WRITER: P.C. VEY

Whatever the age or condition of a house, homeowners will inevitably encounter common problems with their property— things like demon possession, walls dripping blood and dry rot. (Damn that dry rot!) We invite stumped do-it-yourselfers to turn off the House and Garden Channel and submit your questions to our expert…

Dear Mr. Fix-It —

My wife and I are planning to paint the interior of our home. It's a simple job with only one major problem that I can foresee. We keep my grandmother, who is possessed by demons, in one of the upstairs bedrooms. The furniture and my grandmother are constantly flying all over the room, banging into the walls and making a real racket. Also, she constantly spits up all kinds of smelly snot and pus leaving an awful residue on the walls and ceiling. Is there a safe way to paint in such an environment? If so, do you think two coats will be enough? I have enclosed a picture of the smelly snot and pus.

Signed,
Covered in Smelly Snot and Pus

Dear Covered in Smelly Snot and Pus —

Two coats of paint is definitely not enough. Always start with a primer, an undercoat, then two additional coats. In your case I think an oil base paint will have more durability and resist the bodily secretions and potential scuff marks from flying furniture you describe. You are wise to be concerned with safety, as should anyone tackling a home improvement project. You should wear an industrial grade hard hat that meets OSHA requirements. A good pair of ear protectors with a noise reduction rating (NRR) of at least 20 will help drown out most of the ungodly noises and racket. In this situation, you may also want to wear a large Crucifix, especially when working on a ladder.

All The Best, *Mr. Fix-It*

Dear Mr. Fix-It —

My summer house is built over an ancient Indian burial ground. I can put up with the occasional wobbling staircase, moving furniture and nightly wailing of the desecrated spirits, but recently a thick, black, foul-smelling substance has been oozing up through my drains and out of the faucets. You can imagine how hard it is to use the kitchen or bathroom. I've had to cancel several dinner parties as a result. To top it off, the local repair people are all Native Americans and refuse to help me fix the problem. Please find enclosed a snapshot of some of the sludge. I've collected it in one of our wine glasses so as not to have it appear as disgusting as it really is.

Signed, *Baffled in the Country*

Dear Baffled in the Country —

Yours is a common problem. Have a sample of the sludge checked to see if it is merely a backed-up septic tank or the decomposed, violated remains of once-proud indigenous peoples. If it is a septic backup, calling a professional septic tank cleaning service is your easiest solution. Come to think of it, if the sludge is Indian remains, call in the septic tank cleaning service too. That's your name on the deed and you can do with your property whatever you want.

All The Best, *Mr. Fix-It*

Dear Mr. Fix-It —

I recently volunteered the use of my brand new home for a séance with some close friends. Halfway through the proceeding, we actually made contact with the deceased husband of one of the women there. Somehow he knew I had been boinking his wife while his body was still warm in the grave. Well, this guy went medieval all over my recently refinished hardwood floors. He left scrapes, scratches, gouges and some kind of burn marks that smell like sulfur. I don't know how he could do so much damage, since he was barely there being from the spirit world and all. You could see right through him, for Christ's sake! Anyway, the estimate for repair and refinishing was through the roof, which is where my blood pressure is quickly going. Is there a cheap and easy way I can do the job myself? I've enclosed a picture of the guy's grave just to show you he's really dead.

Signed, *Fit To Be Refinished*

Dear Fit To Be Refinished —

Never do things the cheap and easy way. But if you must, a sanding machine can be easily rented at any large hardware or home supply store. Sand with rough (#8), then medium (#12), then fine grit (#15) pads in that order. There should be no problems except for one: rented sanding machines are easily possessed by the spirits of irate dead husbands, or at least behave that way. Make sure whomever conducted the séance properly banished the spirit from your premises, and allow for adequate ventilation in the sanding area. If you plan on having more séances there, consider carpeting.

All The Best, *Mr. Fix-It*

MR. FIX-IT Tackles your Occult and Paranormal Home Repair Problems

Dear Mr. Fix-It —

It was only after I had closed on my house and moved in that I discovered the hot water heater only works on the witches' sabbath. Since, I'm told, there's only a few of them a year, I fear I might have a lifetime of very few showers and dishwashing opportunities. I'm not particularly concerned about the showers, but my dishes were inherited from my mother and have great sentimental value. I just hate to see them gather so much crusty old food. Is there a way to coax the witches to come to my basement more frequently? I've enclosed a photo of the hot water heater.

Signed, *Dirty and Cold*

Dear Dirty and Cold —

Your photo indicates that what you have there is a good old-fashioned cauldron and not a hot water heater at all. I'm guessing you're a first-time homeowner. These days cauldrons are hard to come by and yours looks like it's 100% cast iron. The proper care and maintenance of a cauldron is very time consuming and expensive and could be dangerous if you don't know what you're doing. I suggest you take it to Sears to their Wiccan-goods department and trade it in for a 45 gallon electric water heater — one that isn't filled with newt's eyes and bat's blood. Sears was doing that for a while until the FTC cracked down.

All The Best, *Mr. Fix-It*

Dear Mr. Fix-It —

While repairing some water damage in the basement I found what appeared to be the doorway to Hell. At first I thought it was a door to a root cellar or something, but when I opened the thing...well, you wouldn't believe it! I came face to face with all the pain and suffering of the eternally damned; weeping and gnashing of teeth, a burning agony like I've never seen in my entire life. I'd like to know if there's any way of harnessing some of that energy and directing it into my home heating system? If I can do this I think I might be able to save a bundle on fuel costs this winter. I've enclosed a photo of the door.

Signed, *Soon To Be Toasty Warm*

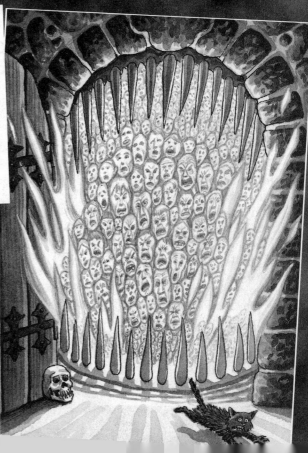

Dear Soon To Be Toasty Warm —

In this era of soaring energy costs and a growing conservation movement, yours is an excellent idea. If you have central heating, the answer may be as simple as running a flexible aluminum heating duct from your newly-found Portal to Hades directly into your system's heat exchanger where it can flow to the vents located throughout your home. If your system is electrically-fired, a solar panel could conceivably convert the energy from the flames licking at the flesh of the everlastingly tormented souls into a virtually inexhaustible supply of usable current. By the way, I think the government offers some substantial tax breaks for those who not only save energy, but use alternative energy sources wisely.

All The Best, *Mr. Fix-It*

Sergio Aragonés Presents A MAD LOOK

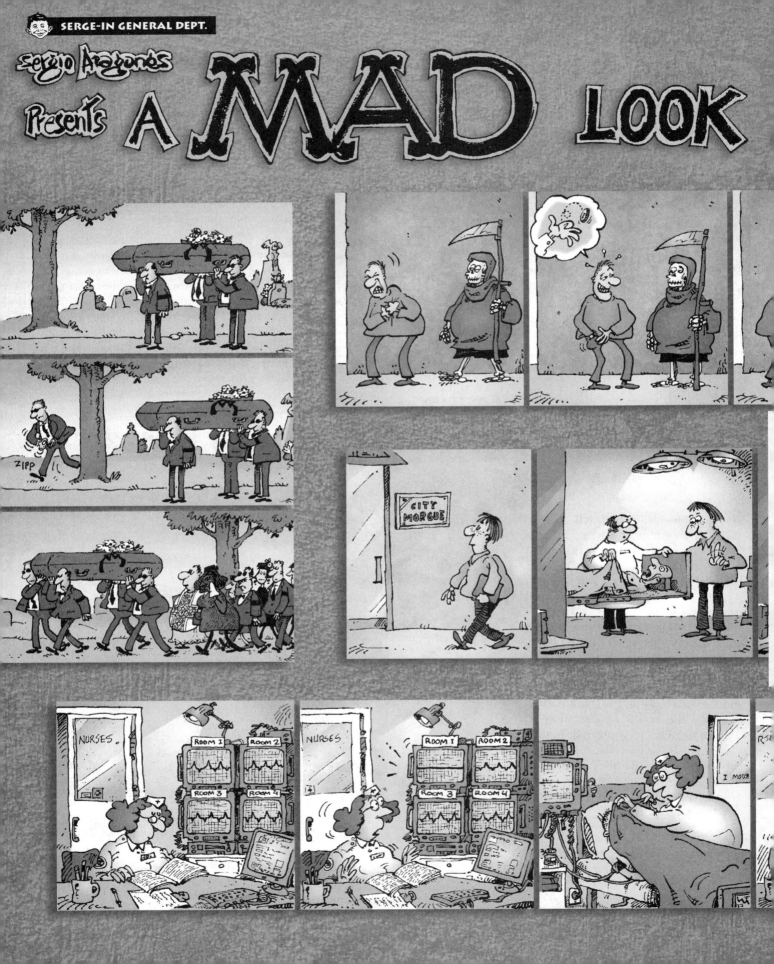

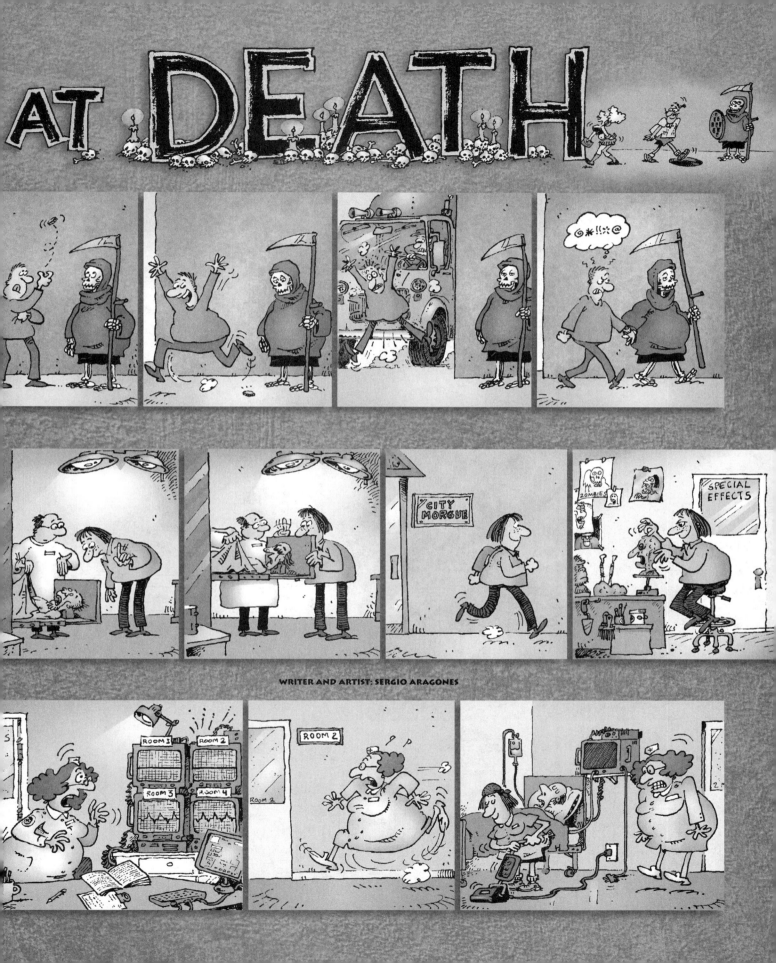

WRITER AND ARTIST: SERGIO ARAGONES

Update the horror classics of the '20s, '30s and '40s and what do you get?... A horror that will never be a classic in any year! Not even when you bring in a guy who fearlessly battles monsters and special effects. No one can save this film, not even...

VAN HEL

ARTIST: TOM RICHMOND WRITER: DICK DEBARTOLO

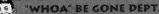

Remember when Keanu Reeves played the focal point of unsuspected multi-dimensional evil trying to break through to everyday existence in *The Devil's Advocate*? How about when he followed that up by playing the focal point of unsuspected multi-dimensional evil trying to break through to everyday existence in *The Matrix*? And, uh, the same focal point in *Matrix Reloaded*? Not to mention *Matrix Revolutions*? So, just how many times is Mr. Excitement going to amble through the exact same part? Judging from his latest devils-and-angels FX-fest, Keanu intends to do it again and again. It's a…

CONS

Hiya! **Satan** here! I'm the **ultimate personification** of **movie evil**! So sorry, **Harvey Weinstein**, you just got **bumped down** to **second place!**

This sullen cardboard cutout is **John Constant-theme**! When Johnny was a **child**, he was declared **clinically dead** for **2 minutes!** After you see his **mumbling performance** in this **film**, you'll say he's got his **record** up to **90!**

Our boy's got **"Pizza Hut Lungs!"** They have a **double crust!** And after the **cancer** gets him, his **soul** belongs to **me. Constant-theme's** headed for a realm of **unending smoke**, and **fire**, and **choking clouds** of **brimstone!** Although, at the pace he **burns** through **cigarettes**, he might not notice the **difference!** When the **Philip Morris Company** had to pay off their **$2.6 billion** anti-smoking settlement, **half** of the money was **profits** they made from **HIM!**

Father Hennessy-On-The-Rocks is a powerful **empath** and an **alcoholic!** His **inner vibrations** lead him to **psychically connect** with a **corpse**, which **brand** him with the same **Satanic symbol** that indicates my son **Moron** is ready to use a **twin psychic** as a fleshy **portal** between **dimensions!** Man, **forget Hennessy-On-The-Rocks!** If I had **my** druthers, they'd run a **breathalyzer** on the guy who **wrote** this **ass-trocious**, convoluted **screenplay!**

The **psychedelic pimp** over here is **Papa Midriff!** As you can see, he spends a lot of time rooting through **Andre 3000's** dumpster for **clothes!** He runs an **eerie establishment** that caters to a clientele of **netherworld freaks** and **weirdos!** It's like an **internet cafe**, only **less seedy!**

ARTIST: HERMANN MEJIA   WRITER: DESMOND DEVLIN

TANT-THEME

This little **chick** with a **nightstick** is **Angina Dudson**! She's a **Los Angeles cop** with a **twin sister**! The **L.A.P.D.** started hiring **identical twins** in **1998!** Smart move! It helps **confuse** the hell out of **juries**, while they're watching **videotaped beatings!**

Everybody in **L.A.** has their own **personal assistant**, but **Spaz Chandler** is just about the **only** one whose **job description** includes **exorcising screeching demonspawn** — that is, other than **Angelina Jolie's** assistant, of course! **Spaz** faces every challenge with **spunk** and **sass!** That's because there's only **one thing** that's **older** than the **ancient curse of the fallen seraphim** — the clichéd, wisecracking **movie sidekick** who **talks "street"!**

I don't want to call **this** one **"ambiguous,"** but she puts the **"bi"** in **"Bible"!** It's **Glockenspiel**, the **angel** with **attitude!** She thinks that **humans** are filthy **creatures** who don't **deserve salvation!** Obviously she's been watching a lot of *Desperate Housewives*!

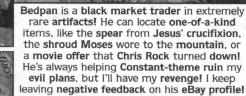

Bedpan is a **black market trader** in extremely rare **artifacts!** He can locate **one-of-a-kind** items, like the **spear** from **Jesus'** crucifixion, the **shroud Moses** wore to the **mountain**, or a **movie offer** that **Chris Rock** turned **down!** He's always helping **Constant-theme** ruin my **evil plans**, but I'll have my **revenge!** I keep leaving **negative feedback** on his **eBay** profile!

Lastly, there's **Howbizarre!** He's one of my **disgruntled employees!** A character that makes a **big splash** before being consigned back to **oblivion!** It was **perfect** casting **Gavin Rossdale** in this role — he's the **lead singer** of **Bush!**

Panel 1: A **computer search** is a good way to find out John Constant-theme's **background**! And it's a **GREAT** way for **lazy-ass screenwriters** to squeeze in sorely-needed **exposition**! Hmmm...I wonder if these **nude photos** of **Satan** were **Photoshopped**? Okay...here he is! **Interests**: standing alone against the **Lord of Darkness** and his army of **demons**! Alone?! So, he's **single**!

Panel 2: **Look** at these **things**! I wish I had The Bug Zapper of Bathsheba!

Panel 3: Are you **sure** you can locate my **sister** in **Hell**, by staring into **Cuddlefuzz's** eyes?

It's **working**! I can feel myself descending into the **fiery realm** of **man's eternal agony**! Either that or Cuddlefuzz is **clawing** my **junk**!

Panel 4: Oh, **this** is more like it! I'm most **definitely** in **Hell** now!

Flee, while you **can**! It's **inhuman**! They're showing the **director's cuts** for **every** screening! Even *Zoolander*!

BEN STILLER & OWEN WILSON FILM FEST

BEN STILLER & OWEN WILSON FILM FESTIVAL

Panel 5: Now I **know** how **Satan's son** plans to enter **Earth**! I must tell John **immediately**! But I have a **compulsion** to drink **every bottle** of **liquor** in this shop! Even though I'm drinking **gallons**, it tastes like **every bottle** is **empty**! Howbizarre's **demonic force** must be **controlling** me! Yeah, the cops'll believe **THAT** one when they **pull me over** for **DUI**!

Tsk, tsk. Shocking behavior from a man of the cloth.

The **sad** thing is, he's only the 3rd most wasted person in here!

Panel 6: Oh no! **Bedpan** is dead and covered in **flies**!

This is **awful**! Just **awful**! I'd assumed that the loud **buzzing noise** when I spoke to **Bedpan** on the **phone** was another **bad connection**! I cancelled my **cell service** for **nothing**!

BUZZ BUZZ BUZZ BUZZ

Panel 7: I hope this **bathtub stunt** helps me **reconnect** with my dormant **psychic abilities**! Do I need to **take off** all my **clothes** for this?

Let me think... no!

Whaddaya mean **NO?!** Ya freakin' **jerk**! Now I hope Satan *does* kick your ass!

Good news! Zombies are making a comeback! It used to be that these creatures were feared and despised by the general population, but no more! Still, don't pop those champagne corks for zombies just yet! Being a zombie ain't easy, as you'll see in...

JOHN CALDWELL'S
THINGS THAT REALLY GET UNDER A ZOMBIE'S SKIN

WRITER AND ARTIST: JOHN CALDWELL

The fact that, no matter how hard he tries, he's never among the first 100 patrons to get something for free

Picnic ants

When, just before a big date, his face breaks out in nightcrawlers

Flip–flopping government studies saying one day that eating brains lowers cholesterol, then the next day, declaring just the opposite

The seemingly insurmountable problems associated with getting a barbed wire bicep tattoo

That debilitating variety of erectile dysfunction that's unique to zombies

Getting Punk'd

Seriously mis–timing that hand–popping–out–from–the–grave moment

It's easy to make a wildly entertaining summer blockbuster! Take a thrilling script, add a captivating leading man, throw in some creepy crop circles and— bammo! — you've got a hit! But, what if the story is the umpteenth knock-off of *Close Encounters of the Third Kind*? And what if your star looks like he just woke from a 14-month nap? And what if the crop circles were lame after the 100th preview? Then you've got problems — and the studio's got nothing but a 2-hour dud filled with their painfully failed…

desig

I keep **waking up** in the **middle** of the **night** with a terrible feeling **something** is **wrong**. It's almost as if I have a *Sixth Sense* that some-thing **bad** is happening in my **corn-fields**! I've been so **edgy** since my **wife died**. I **blame God** for **taking** her, but I **suppose** the **guy** in the **truck** who **mowed her down** didn't exactly **help**! When she **passed on**, I decided **there is no God**! **That's** when I **left** my position as **Minister at Saint Dubious**!

When my **brother** lost his wife, he went into a **deep depression**, so **I** moved up here to **be with him**. Since **I** got here, a **big problem's** developed. His **kids** seem to **like me** more than **him**! **I guess** it's because I pay **more attention** to them, and that I care **enough** about them to **learn their first names**! I'm a touch **depressed**, too. I've been **unable** to **find employment** in my **specialized field** of "failed baseball players"! I was a **star slugger**, then one day my **baseball career** was suddenly **over**. I guess a 6-foot, 24-year-old weighing **200 pounds** can **fool Little League officials** for only **so long**! **Damn**!

We woke up this morning and found these **huge designs** in our **cornfield**. I **told** my dad I thought **God did it**. My dad said God probably **did** do it, because God has plenty of **time** on his **hands** to **screw around**, now that he **no longer chooses to answer people's prayers**!

I HATE CORN…

MAX KORN FIELD

When the **voices** told me *"build it and they will come,"* I **thought** they meant **fans**, not **aliens**!

It's **true**! When you're **near death**, your life **flashes before your eyes**. I see that **lonely farmhouse** my husband **made** me move into, a **million miles** from **civilization**. I see me watering a **hundred acres** of corn with a **bucket**. Wow, even my **flashback** seems **dreary**! Maybe I should *thank* the guy who **drove the truck** that **hit me** and got me **out** of this **rural hellhole**!

Of all the **bad luck**! I ran down the **minister's wife**! **Why** did that have to **happen**? **God** is going to **take vengeance** on me! **Why** couldn't I have been **lucky** and **run over** the **wife** of an **atheist**!

SILLY SCREEN PLAYS

CORNY SCRIPT

ARTIST: ANGELO TORRES   WRITER: DICK DEBARTOLO

The do-it-yourselfer faces a wide variety of gruesome and ungodly characters — bloodthirsty ghouls, undead specters from beyond, even licensed contractors. But before you douse yourself in holy water and roll up yours sleeves for the hellish task at hand, see if our own expert can offer some help...

MORE MR. FIX-IT
Tackles Your
OCCULT And PARANORMAL
HOME REPAIR PROBLEMS

Dear Mr. Fix-It,

My new roommate, Vlad, is a vampire. However, his coffin is very old, and the joints are dried out and loosening. With the drapes open, it provides little protection from the sun and he makes quite a racket, restlessly tossing in his unholy slumber. Because of the coffin's disrepair, the curtains have to be drawn all day long, even though it is depressing and causing my plants to die.

Is there a simple and easy way I can tighten up his squeaky coffin so he won't make so much noise when I try to enjoy the sun? I'm afraid if this problem continues, he'll be left defenseless against the light and his body will horribly collapse into a steaming, hissing mass of putrid decay. This would be a shame, since he always pays his half of the rent on time and good roommates are hard to find.

I've enclosed a photo of Vlad with one of his latest victims. You can see the coffin in the background.

Signed,
Dying to Get Some Quiet

ARTIST: JAMES WARHOLA
WRITER: P.C. VEY

Dear Dying to Get Some Quiet,

You might have a bigger problem than you think. Most vampiric coffins are made from a specific kind of black oak found only in the most remote regions of the Carpathian Forest. This wood is chosen specifically for its hardness, durability and, in most cases, impenetrability. In essence, you couldn't drive a screw into it if all the lost souls taken by all the blood-sucking hordes throughout history depended on it. You could try glue and clamps, though. Plain old Elmer's glue would do the trick — adding a little ground garlic will loosen up the wood and make it a bit easier to force it back into its unholy original shape. Be careful not to use too much garlic though, as you might have one angry vampire on your hands.

After applying the glue, use as many three and six-foot C-clamps as it takes to slowly squeeze the joints together. Make sure to use some pieces of soft wood (like pine) as cushions between the clamps and the coffin. It would really be a shame to mar the finish of such an ancient and diabolical piece of workmanship.

All the best, Mr. Fix-It

Dear Mr. Fix-It,

I recently laid some beautiful Spanish tiles in my kitchen. They really look great but I suspect the adhesive I used was not right for the job. Not two days after I thought I was finished, the tiles started moving around. I don't mean slipping out of place due to foot traffic, I mean crashing around the house, leaving incredible mayhem and destruction in their wake. After a week, every single tile relocated itself to a different part of the house and rested in the rubble and dust that I once called home. I even found one in the crib. Thank God we don't have a baby.

When I called the store where I bought the product, all I heard were blood-curdling screams and someone yelling in the background about a man-eating, putty-colored blob that was mistakenly packaged as floor and tile adhesive. It's been two weeks now and the inside of my house has gone from bad to worse. And I've nearly been eaten *twice*. What should I do?

I've enclosed a photo of the container it came in and what used to be my kitchen.

Signed, Food For Adhesive

Dear Food For Adhesive,

Putty can make a real mess if not handled properly. First, you should put on a pair of heavy-duty industrial rubber gloves and a plastic helmet with a clear shield for your face. Then, carefully scrape off as much blob as you can from the tiles and dispose of it. Use a reinforced airtight hazardous materials container and have somebody from the EPA come and pick it up. Whatever you do, don't just throw it in the trash or dump it in a lake. If it got into the ground water, it could easily kill every man, woman and child in your community.

After the tiles are nice and clean, get some quality (and yes, costly) floor and tile adhesive, apply it in a thick, even coat to the back of each tile and set them firmly into place. It never pays to skimp on materials — but if the product was defective and was, in fact, a man-eating blob rather than the floor adhesive it claimed to be, a strongly-worded letter to the manufacturer should get you a full refund.

All the best, Mr. Fix-It

Dear Mr. Fix-It,

The devil is living in my refrigerator. I know it's Satan himself and not some lesser demon, because I signed a pact with him 15 years ago and one of the sub-clauses stated that he could live in my refrigerator if he wanted to. At the time I thought nothing of it. After all, why in hell would Satan want to live in my refrigerator? It's an older model and the compressor is just about shot. But apparently I was wrong and now I'm paying the price. Nothing stays cold anymore. Dairy products just go putrid. Fruits and vegetables sit in a pool of their own self-emanating slime. All my leftovers are covered with a multicolored fungus that I swear shows some signs of intelligence. At times, the thing radiates so much heat I have to open the windows, which let in the thousands of flies that seem to gather outside the house on a daily basis. I called a refrigerator repairman but he says he doesn't work on satanic appliances. The best he could recommend was canned foods or take-out. I've enclosed a photo of my kitchen.

Signed, Eating Out A Lot

Dear Eating Out A Lot,

Your first mistake was signing anything with the devil, let alone a pact. Try consulting the warranty to see if the manufacturer covers the problem. If it doesn't, just unplug the thing, and bring it out to your front lawn for the trash. Old appliances, satanic or otherwise, are usually not worth repairing. When buying yourself a new refrigerator, be sure to use a fake ID and a clever disguise. If your pact with the devil is airtight — and most of them are — he'll move right into the new one if he knows you bought it. Of course, you could always move to a much colder climate, say, somewhere along the Arctic Circle, where you could easily get along without a refrigerator. But then you might always wonder if he'll show up demanding to move into an old ice chest or some cold beverage insulator.

All the best, Mr. Fix-It

Dear Mr. Fix-It,

I have hundreds of rampaging, zombie beetles burrowing their way through my house right now. Normally this kind of thing wouldn't bother me, but I'm trying to put up some sheetrock in the basement and my home is falling apart around me. I've tried a protective jumpsuit and special goggles that my optometrist prescribed, but they only seem to anger the swarm of insects. Their destruction and bloodlust have already caused me to nail two fingers and a thumb to the wall by mistake. How can I finish this job I started? I've enclosed a badly taken photo of myself trying to cope — because it's also hard to use a camera in this condition.

Signed, Up Against a Wall

Dear Up Against a Wall,

You should ask a friend or neighbor to help — putting up sheetrock is really a two man job, even in ideal situations. If your predicament has alienated all your friends and scared off all your neighbors, you could always hire a handyman. They don't charge much and are good workers. Additionally, most are second-rate professional carpenters who want to get in, do the job and get out without much conversation or judgment, no matter what kind of peculiar situation presents itself. This seems perfect in your case.

Remember to use waterproof sheetrock screws, as blood will rust regular screws as easily as water.

All the best, Mr. Fix-It

Dear Mr. Fix-It,

I believe my house is being targeted by flying saucers. The other day, a formation of six swooped down and rattled my roof so hard, some of the shingles flew off and my chimney shook so much I thought it was going to collapse. Then, last night, nine of them buzzed around my house for an hour, taking turns bumping into it. As a result, some bricks actually did fall from the chimney, one right down the flue, hitting me in the face as I was looking up it to get a better look. I realize this isn't the end of the world, as some of my UFO books would indicate, but I have a genuine fear that the chimney might actually fall over during the next big rainstorm.

Is there any way I can shore it up or strengthen it so it might last the lifetime it was guaranteed to last?

Signed, Still Bleeding From the Brick

Dear Still Bleeding From the Brick,

I wish you had sent me a photo of your chimney. It's hard to help you if I'm left in the dark as to the extent of damage done. However, if it has been bombarded in this way and lost a number of bricks, I would have to think the integrity of its structure has been compromised — in which case, you may need a whole new one built. My advice to you is not to do the job yourself. A job like this, done incorrectly, could give you even bigger trouble later on down the line.

But, if you insist on tackling the job yourself, avoid using lumber — it could ignite during your next sighting. I wouldn't rebuild it with bricks either, as you will probably just have the same experience during the next big onslaught. Reinforced concrete encased in an inch of plate steel might be a good idea. It will be tricky getting it up to your roof, but a military contractor probably has some expertise with this sort of thing. Try contacting your local army base for help.

All the best, Mr. Fix-It

sergio Aragonés presents a MAD look at

the twilight saga

WRITER AND ARTIST: SERGIO ARAGONÉS   COLORIST: TOM LUTH

Hey, gang! It's time once again for MAD's nutty old "Cliché Monster" game. Here's how it works: Take any familiar phrase or colloquial expression, give it an eerie setting so you create a new-type monster, and you're playing it. Mainly, you're—

HORRIFYING CLICHÉS

ARTIST: PAUL COKER, JR.   WRITER: MAY SAKAMI

Springing A TRAP

Padding An EXPENSE ACCOUNT

Redeeming A COUPON

Committing A CRIME

Drafting An AGREEMENT

Changing An OPINION

Awakening An INTEREST

Making An EDUCATED GUESS

Filling A VOID

Pressing For An ANSWER

Analyzing A SITUATION

Unraveling A MYSTERY

Unseating An INCUMBENT

Spiking A DRINK

Tripping the LIGHT FANTASTIC

Balancing A BUDGET

Here's the show that stars Michael C. Hall, the guy from Six Feet Under! On that show, he could talk with people who had just died. On this show, he speaks with people who are about to die! We guess that's a step up in some perverse way! On this series there's so much mutilation and gore, the producers thought of calling it Dissects and the City! *Spoiler alert: maybe you've only seen the first season, but (and don't kill us now) we're taking on the first two seasons of…*

I'm **Deathster Morgue'in**…I **kill** people…**lots** of people! **Inside**, I'm a **raging storm** of **darkness**… the **gloomy fog** of **despair clouds** my **vision**… a **flood** of **moody melancholy rains** upon me…with **narration** like **that**, you're probably **wondering** why I don't work at **The Weather Channel! Killing** is **part** of me! Sometimes I work **fast** but most times I'm **slow** and **methodical** — for instance, you see these **donuts** I always bring in for my **co-workers?** They're **loaded** with **trans fat!** Let me introduce the **crew!**

That's **Detective Angel Badteaser!** He's **great**, especially in cases involving **Miami's** large **Cuban** and **Latino** population! You know, I **love** the **Spanish language**, the **words** sound so **romantic** to me…**muerte, machete, violencia!**

When I work **undercover**, no one **suspects** I'm a **cop** — that's because of my **tacky wardrobe!** On my **meager police salary**, even the **homeless** have **better clothes** than me! Working **murder investigations** with **Deathster** is…how shall I put it **delicately**… **friggin' weird!** I once told him I read that the **five stages** of dealing with **death** are **Denial, Anger, Bargaining, Depression** and **Acceptance**. He told me **his** five stages of dealing with **death** are **Anticipation, Happiness, Joy, Ecstasy** and **Orgasm!**

That **picture** is my **foster dad, Scary Morgue'in!** He was a **brilliant policeman** and a **kind, decent** and **loving father**. When he realized I exhibited the **tendencies** of a **serial killer**, he did what **any good cop** would do: he taught me to **blend in** and **hide** my **aberration** so I could go on **killing** for **decades! Thanks, Dad!**

Here's **Sgt. Croakes!** He's the **only member** of the force **creeped out** by me! Can he sense the **Dark Passenger** within me? The **curtain** that hangs over my **soul**, with a matching **valence** of **anguish** and **emptiness?** Of course, a **simpler explanation** would be he just doesn't like **white guys!**

What Deathster **doesn't know** is I have some **secrets** of my **own!** I'm a former **Special Ops officer** and I've seen some pretty **violent** and **disturbing events**, like the first **Gulf War, Haitian coups**, and the **worst** of all, when **Miami** was **flooded** with **Young Republicans** during the **2000 Florida Presidential vote recount! THAT** was **ugly!**

That's **Vince Masukka** — my fellow **forensics expert**, as well as a **horny, foul-mouthed, gross, inappropriate-comment-making geek!** Think of him as the **Manga** version of **Beavis** and **Butt-head!**

SERGIO ARAGONES PRESENTS A MAD LOOK AT ZOMBIES

WRITER AND ARTIST: SERGIO ARAGONES

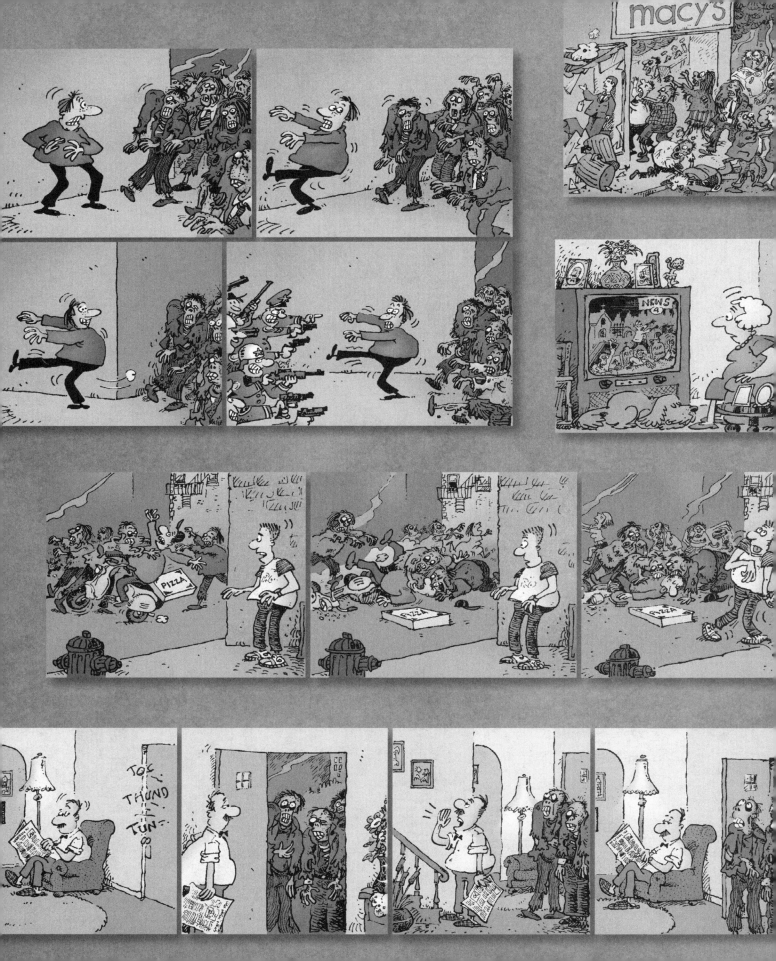

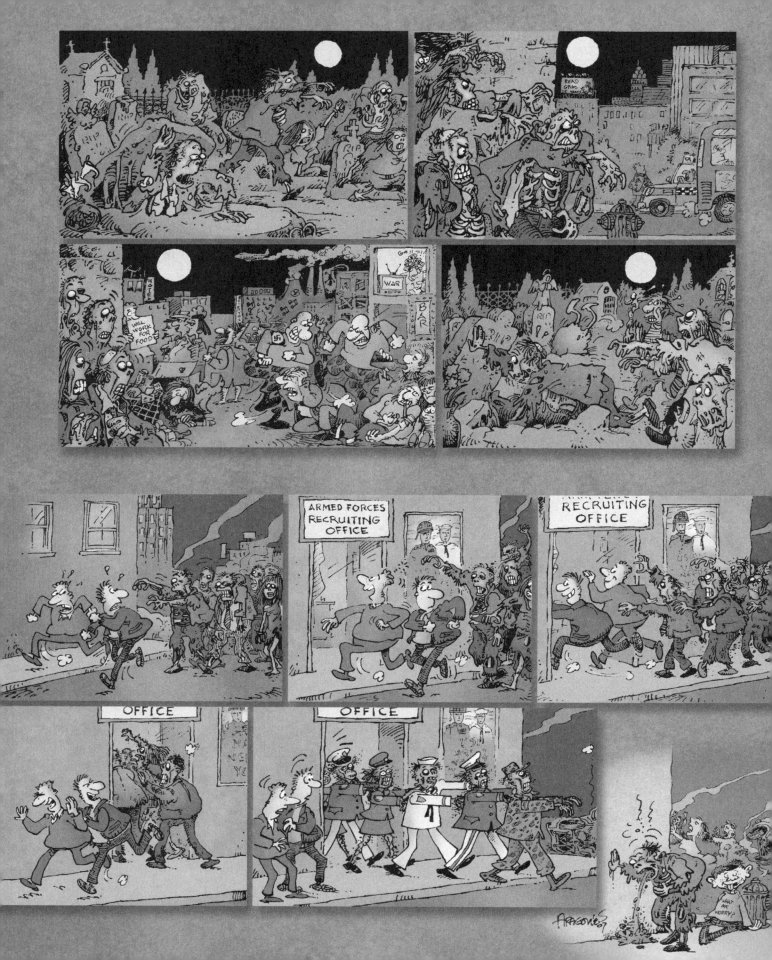